TURN TOWARD PROMISE

TURN
TOWARD
PROMISE

THE PROPHETS
AND SPIRITUAL RENEWAL

JOHN INDERMARK

UPPER
ROOM BOOKS®
NASHVILLE

Cover design: Lecy Design
Cover landscape image: Richard T. Nowitz / National Geographic Image Collection / Getty Images
Interior design and implementation: Nancy Cole-Hatcher
First printing: 2004

Library of Congress Cataloging-in-Publication
Indermark, John, 1950-
Turn toward promise : the prophets and spiritual renewal / John Indermark.
p. cm.
ISBN 0-8358-9887-3
1. Spiritual formation. 2. Bible. O.T. Isaiah—Meditations. 3. Bible. O.T. Jeremiah—Meditations. 4. Bible. O.T. Ezekiel—Meditations. I. Title.
BV4511.I52 2004
242'.5—dc22   2004011373

To

DR. WALTER BRUEGGEMANN

who opened the prophetic word to me in seminary

who opened the first door in my pursuit of a ministry of writing

who has been for this generation,
whether in agreement or disagreement
with his teachings and advocacies,
an embodiment of Ezekiel 2:5:

"They shall know that there has been a prophet among them."

Contents

✦

Acknowledgments

A BOOK IS A collaboration. Literally. The labors are shared by many hands and eyes beyond those of the author. The good folks at Upper Room Books continue to be valued partners in my practice of ministry through the written word. JoAnn Miller provided suggestions that strengthened the focus of this work at an early stage. As project editor, Jeannie Crawford-Lee greatly increased clarity of word and thought as she guided this manuscript through the revision process. Sarah Schaller-Linn and Denise Duke lent their expertise to issues of verification and copyright.

Closer to home, I have been blessed with colleagues and family whose share in the labors of this book have taken many forms. The writing group I participate in has evolved into a writing triad. Brian Harrison and Jenelle Varila have walked the writing path with me for a number of years. They have strengthened my work over time through careful listening, clear critiquing, and steady friendship. The emotional (and financial!) support I have needed to exercise the vocation of writing is given by my wife, Judy Wilson Indermark. She graces my life with love and encouragement that have made this ministry possible from the very start. While writing and then editing this book, I have been privileged to coauthor two study books for young adults with my son, Jeff Indermark. That experience has been a gift lending energy to this project.

Finally, I am glad to acknowledge my indebtedness in *Turn Toward Promise* to Dr. Walter Brueggemann. A letter from him at the outset of this project encouraged me to pursue it as well as underscored the need to hold in tension issues of personal spiritual formation with societal transformation. Beyond that letter, several of Dr. Brueggemann's books provided constant companions during times of research and then writing. *The Prophetic Imagination* and *Cadences of Hope* offered compelling and powerful overviews of the prophetic word's function in Israel and in our time. His commentaries on Jeremiah (Eerdmans) and Isaiah (Westminster/John Knox Press) faithfully unpacked passages specific to this book, both in exegetical understanding and contemporary application. If you wish to further your own studies into the prophets, you could do no better than to begin with these books.

I am also glad to acknowledge that my first deep encounters with the prophets came in an 8:00 AM course taught by Dr. Brueggemann in a basement classroom of the Eden Seminary/Webster University Library. I say "taught" advisedly, because lectures there more closely resembled sermons. In one sense, this book's attempt to fuse the prophetic message with issues of spiritual formation simply carries on what happened in that 8:00 AM hour. For not only did the classes take form in Dr. Brueggemann's unique style of teaching and preaching, but those classes and countless ones since were opened with prayer. A portion of one such prayer, offered January 13, 1994 at Columbia Theological Seminary, serves as a fitting transition from acknowledgments to task at hand:

> *Form us in freedom and wholeness and gentleness.*
> *Reform our deformed lives toward*
>   *obedience which is our only freedom,*
>   *praise which is our only poetry,*
>   *and love which is our only option.*

And let the people of God say, Amen and Amen!

✦

Before You Begin

THE PROPHETS AND SPIRITUAL RENEWAL

Consider the following two statements. Do either—or both—ring true for you? (1) You have an interest in spiritual formation. (2) You have an interest in how the prophets of Israel address persons and communities today.

Turn Toward Promise intends to lead you on a journey that explores the interrelationships between those two elements of faith for individuals and communities. Passages from Isaiah, Jeremiah, and Ezekiel will provide the signposts for that exploration. These and other prophets traditionally have been read and interpreted in ways that emphasize their witness to Israel as a political, social, and religious community. Their words and visions exercise a necessary voice in calling communities to accountability where social and political imbalances occur. Interests in exploring personal dynamics have been largely limited to concerns about the prophets as individuals (for example, Jeremiah's personal anguish or the nature of Ezekiel's visions).

Turn Toward Promise takes a slightly different approach. It draws on the words and images of these prophets to engage you and others today with the invitation to spiritual renewal. *Turn* is the first word of the title because, whether for individuals or communities, spiritual renewal always involves change and redirection. The nature of such transformation, which the prophets sought for the community of Israel, bears fascinating possibilities for disciplines of personal spiritual formation. This emphasis does not at all lessen the prophetic demands for justice and right relationships addressed to the larger communities and societies in which persons live. Indeed, you will find those other core elements of the prophetic word irresistibly making their way into this work—and into your life—time and again. It cannot be otherwise. "Spiritual formation for individuals never happens in a vacuum, but it happens in a social context," according to Walter Brueggemann. *Turn Toward Promise* simply seeks to hear those prophetic voices summon individuals as well as communities to transformation.

SUGGESTIONS FOR USING THIS BOOK

Two introductions, one for the first three weeks and another for the second three weeks, provide background material to set these prophets in their historical context. Please read the introductions before you start the weekly readings. These introductions also may assist you in making connections between the biblical texts and the settings in which you live.

Once you are ready to begin the weekly readings, look over the structure of the book. *Turn Toward Promise* is intended to be read over a six-week period. Each week offers six readings: one per day, with a seventh-day "sabbath" from reading. If you are reading this book as part of a group study, organize your daily reading so that the seventh day free of readings falls on the day or evening of your group meeting.

Each daily reading consists of a biblical reference and brief quotation from one of the prophets, a meditation on the text, a prayer, and a spiritual exercise. Please read the scripture passage first. It sets the stage for the reflective piece to follow. And do not neglect to do the daily Spiritual Exercises. They are intended to connect each day's theme with your own spiritual journey and growth.

Find a time of day when you can do the daily readings with adequate opportunity to focus upon these words and what they speak to you. Unless there are extenuating circumstances, do not try to cram a whole week's readings into one day. Be patient. Let each day's reading be sufficient for that day. Allow the content and reflection to build over the course of days.

JOURNALING

One consistent component through the daily exercises involves journaling. For some of you, this will be nothing new. Many people have come to practice journaling as a regular discipline of spiritual reflection. But do not be concerned if you have never journaled before in your life. The exercises provide specific instruction, so you need not invent a process yourself. Nor should you feel as though there is only one right way to journal. There is not. Journaling as used in these exercises simply invites you to keep a written record of ideas, reflections, and prayers. For ease of reference, particularly if you do this as part of a group, use a notebook or binder to keep journal pages in order. Consider dating the entries or headlining them with week and day numbers.

Whether this discipline of journaling is new or old, allow it to lead you deeper not only into the texts but into yourself and ultimately deeper into your relationship with God.

✦
Introduction to Weeks 1–3

In 722 BCE, the armies of Assyria swept through the northern kingdom of Israel. The capital, Samaria, fell; its king, Hoshea, was imprisoned; and the peoples of the ten northern tribes were either killed or resettled. The so-called "lost tribes" of Israel refer to the untraced disappearance of this population. In 597 BCE, the Chaldean (Babylonian) Empire under Nebuchadnezzar overran the southern kingdom of Judah and took control of Jerusalem. It deported a portion of its population to Babylon, including the king, to insure obedience. A new king was set in place, but his participation in a rebellion against the Babylonians resulted in Jerusalem's destruction in 587. The deportation or dispersion of the remaining population came to be known as the Exile.

Such brief historical facts do not nearly do justice to the era that preceded and included the prophets' activity. However they do introduce the crises that formed the backdrop for the works of Isaiah, Jeremiah, and Ezekiel.

Precisely at this point, you may wonder: *So what? That happened in a place and time far distant from my home and to peoples I have never known; what has that to do with me? What has that to do with my relationship to a wider society and culture vying for my allegiance and thoughts in ways that feel at times remarkably religious in tone and claim? What has that to do with the community of faith in which I am immersed or entangled or something in between? What has that to do with deepening my spiritual walk with and by God?*

Such questions home in on the perennial task of encountering biblical texts: connecting the texts to life and faith and witness today. This book invites you to find echoes of your fears and hopes, wonderings and struggles, in these prophetic texts. And in finding those echoes, this book challenges you to let that prophetic word form you as a person of faith turned toward the promises of God.

The themes of these opening weeks reflect movements of spiritual transformation vital in our lives as well as integral to the messages of Isaiah, Jeremiah, and Ezekiel. "Confronting a New Reality" asks us to consider that the purposes of God often run counter to conventional wisdom of the day. "Casting Off Illusions" calls on us to distinguish between what is real and what is illusory in our life in general and our faith in particular. "Speaking Truth to Power" reminds us how the prophetic message challenges powers and authorities that overstate their claims on our lives. Each week, we will explore texts that once evoked transformation on the part of Israel and still bid individuals and communities to such change. Allow these texts to bring their perspectives on renewal to your own experiences, hopes, and perhaps fears.

Consider, for example, that those whom these prophets originally addressed could not see or would not admit what was coming. Has that ever been a dynamic at work in your life? Have you ever seen such denial or obliviousness in the community in which you live, conduct business, or engage in worship? Isaiah, Jeremiah, and Ezekiel offered words at odds with the prevailing culture in order to disrupt it with new possibilities and challenges. Spiritual formation carries that same edge to it. The working of God's Spirit relies on a willingness to be formed in new ways. More often than not, that transformation begins with movements and actions that would not have been our first choice had we been calling the shots.

"Judgment" can rightly convey the meaning of such disruption and its invitation to change.

The reasons the prophets' words came across as contrarian then—and why they may still find resistance today—are varied. Isaiah, and to some degree Jeremiah, offered these words in times of relative peace and prosperity. Distant threats can be put at even greater distance when they do not immediately impact the status quo. Ezekiel prophesied to a community already in exile. Even then, Ezekiel's audience denied the nature and extent of the crisis. Consider modern voices that trouble prosperous and contented communities, churches, nations, or persons with unwanted words. Racism lurks. Social and economic inequities divide. Natural resources dwindle because of the shortsightedness of their stewards. Religion dwells on superficial matters. When life goes well, nobody wants to hear about such troubling issues, certainly not when they upset our habitual way of doing things. If we just think good thoughts and eliminate all the negative talk, crises will pass without our having to change. So the rationale went then, and so it still goes in some places.

Israel's religious identity contributed in this era to a sense of false well-being. Had God not chosen Israel as God's people and this place as our land? God would allow no significant harm to come to those set apart. Surely there would be deliverance, if need be, as there had been from Egypt! Then as now, religious self-assuredness results in stiff resistance to transformation and change.

The political and military situation for Israel grew more hazardous in the latter years of the eighth century BCE and again at the close of the seventh century. As a result, those in power in Israel wrangled for alliances with neighbors. They reasoned the preservation of land and freedom depended on throwing in their lot with the most favorable military coalition. In contrast, Isaiah, Jeremiah, and Ezekiel declared the future could not be guaranteed by pulling together the biggest military coalition on the block. The future belonged to God. Most of you reading this book probably do not sit in the inner chambers of national power. So it might seem this part of the prophetic word gives you (and me) a pass. Then again, the exercise of power and even coercion is not limited to heads of state. People use power in relationships, in the conduct of business, within families, and yes, even in churches. Prophetic judgment still weighs in against power rooted in the equivalent of "might makes right." The exercise of power remains a critical concern in spiritual formation. If you wonder about the validity of that statement, revisit Jesus' admonition to disciples angry about James and John's request for privileged positions of power (Mark 10:42-44).

Isaiah, Jeremiah, and Ezekiel brought announcements of God's judgment to bear on the crises they perceived in their times. In his *Theology of the Old Testament*, Walter Brueggemann makes the critical point that the prophets not only understand their eras as presenting crisis. At times the prophets provoke the crisis. On people quite willing to ignore any need for change, much less acknowledge change already at work, the prophets insist that judgment will fall. God will do what God will do. The prophetic task of judgment required announcing beginnings and endings wrought by God. Isaiah, Jeremiah, and Ezekiel did not shy away from revealing that Israel was poised on the edge of a season largely defined by endings.

Making connections between modern-day conditions and these ancient prophetic works involves acknowledging that God is and will be sovereign in history and in life. The crisis born of judgment confesses that all may not be as it should be in life, both public and private. God remains free to address that unsettling truth as God chooses in the lives of communities as well as persons. God even may be at work when long-standing institutions are shaken, including those that routinely invoke the name of God.

Yet crisis can become opportunity. Words of judgment offer the possibility of not only disrupting life as it is but also reforming life toward what God seeks it to be. So the prophets addressed Israel then, and so they address us today: in hope of reordering how we live in response to the presence of God. God seeks our transformation as individuals and as communities of faith. But in order for such turning toward God's promises to take place, we need to confront what is unreal, deceitful, and oppressive in our midst. That is where the journey of turning must first take us, so that the hope of God's promise may be distinguished from mere wishful thinking.

WEEK ONE

Confronting
a New Reality

DAY I

Vineyards and Wild Grapes

ISAIAH 5:1-7

My beloved had a vineyard . . . he expected it to yield grapes,
but it yielded wild grapes.—Isaiah5:1-2

DEEPLY RELIGIOUS AND loving parents raise a child who inexplicably causes them no end of grief. Bad companions. Worse choices. The natural development toward independence degenerates into a bitter rebellion that rebuffs every effort to offer help. The child seems to remember and push only the buttons to get money for who knows what. The mystery of this spiraling catastrophe only deepens when another child reared in that same family exhibits none of those tendencies. What went wrong—and what to do?

"Let me sing for my beloved my love-song concerning his vineyard." The intimacy of such language underscores the almost familial tie that linked vineyard to vinedresser in ancient Israel. A vineyard passed from generation to generation within the same family. Like a child, the vineyard required significant hands-on nurture: pruning the branches, turning the soil beneath the vine. When harvest neared, the owner or workers often moved into a shelter in the vineyard to keep constant watch over the ripening crop.

Typically a new vine took at least four years to set its first fruit. So imagine yourself tending such a vine from inception.

Before the planting can take place, you must remove rocks by hand, often stacking them into walls intended to keep out danger. Young vines require careful watering during the dry seasons. Trimming and hoeing occupy those same early years. You work with patience. You wait in hopeful expectation of first harvest. Then, at last, fruit begins to form and swell on the vine. You rejoice, then you grieve. The long-desired crop proves to be a wild variety of no worth. Years of waiting, years of hoping, years of working, have gone to ruin.

Isaiah's parable does not mince words in its ensuing declaration of judgment. The crisis, however, is not so much the shocking declaration in verses 5–6 of what God will do but why God will act. God "expected justice, but saw bloodshed; righteousness, but heard a cry!" (v. 7). Sometimes only extreme statements will shake individuals and communities out of complacency, out of illusion confused with reality. Sometimes even those statements do not suffice to bring about the needed change—whether with unruly vineyards, root-bound traditions, or wandering loved ones.

The parable's sternness might seem an unduly ominous text at the beginning of a book aimed at transformation. Spiritual formation is about possibilities and hope, isn't it? True enough. Yet the prophetic tradition also prepares persons and communities for transformation precisely by naming the need for change. Isaiah here points out what risks judgment if change is not forthcoming. Actions have consequences. Calling brings vocation. The God of justice, mercy, and love bids us into covenant. The prophets insist that relationship with such a God invites us to evidence that same justice, mercy, and love in our lives.

Now some of you may be saying: *I thought this was a book about spiritual formation, about the inner life forged in relationship with God.* It is. But the prophets also reveal that we cannot practice our relationship with God in isolation from conduct of our public lives. Spiritual transformation, in the light of Isaiah's parable, does not exhaust itself in warmed hearts and time-honored devotional practices. Spiritual transformation also unfolds in the doing of justice, the loving of mercy, and the walking humbly with God (see Micah 6:8).

Isaiah's song of the vineyard invites you to discover what such transformation might mean for you and for the communities in which you live and worship, raise children and cast votes, relax in leisure and engage in service. What stands there in need of uprooting or pruning in order for a new harvest of justice and righteousness to take root?

> *God, are there ways I have lost sight of you—of your justice, of your compassion? Do my spirit and my life bear the fruit you truly seek? Help me. Nurture me. Transform me. Amen.*

SPIRITUAL EXERCISE

Read over the parable of the vineyard several times. Listen for how it speaks today: to you, to your faith community. Reflect on what possibly might or already does impede your relationship with God as well as your interaction with others. In your journal, identify this issue and brainstorm ideas as to how you might, with God's help, work at changing or transforming it. Be at prayer about this tonight and in the coming days.

DAY 2

✦

Closure

ISAIAH 6:9-13

Stop their ears . . . shut their eyes.—Isaiah 6:10

ISAIAH 6 HAS long fed attentive readers with food for thought and spirit. We feel ourselves drawn to its opening eight verses, culminating in the prophet's response: "Here am I; send me!" For many sermons and encounters with this text, the chapter would seem to end here. Stopping at that point, however, omits the prophet's commissioning in verses 9–13: "Make the mind of this people dull . . . stop their ears . . . shut their eyes." Why? What forms the rationale for such a harsh calling that would make sure this people do not "turn and be healed"?

You may want to stop and read (or reread) Isaiah 6:9-13. It is an astounding word. It is exactly what you would not expect of God, perhaps the best clue that it *is* a true word of God. Hard but true. For the word announces closure. Verses 9–10 suggest that God does not even *want* a possibility of turning. God commissions the prophet to tell hearers to keep looking and listening for the word the prophet speaks—just so long as they don't get it!

Is this reverse psychology in which God baits Israel with the equivalent of "Don't bother" so that they will bother? That would be a clever answer to a difficult problem. Unfortunately nothing in the text suggests such a resolution to the dilemma posed by God. At this point, the one who cried out, "Here am I; send me" now finds the terms of sending cause for questioning. "How long, O LORD?" Isaiah asks. Those words echo in Israel's psalms of lament and complaint that ask how long the cause of pain or threat to life will be allowed to endure. Those words still echo where persons walk in suffering, endure oppression, or experience injustice: *How long?* It is a fair and faithful question to ask.

Then again, one ought not to ask questions for which one is not prepared to hear the answer. Isaiah's "how long?" finds reply in the pronouncement of closure's reality: cities in waste without inhabitants, the land desolate—even its remnants subject to burning. Devastation.

Isaiah rivals the bleakness of Amos in these words of judgment. At the core of this judgment lies an image of God very different from what we are used to affirming, much less celebrating. The God here revealed to Israel and to us at times says, "No more." Points of no return can be reached. Perhaps we hope that truth resides in distance *we* place between ourselves and God's purposes. We would hope that it is not God who shuts the door or says the final no. We would prefer to believe we ourselves dull our minds, stop our ears, shut our eyes rather than God's imposing such closures on us. Maybe that explains why we don't often hear Isaiah 6:9-13 read from pulpits or printed on religious greeting cards. We want God always ready for us, no matter how long or late we are to see or hear or turn.

Isaiah 6:9-13 provides no easy answers. It holds out the sobering possibility that times may well come when rebirth must be preceded by the leveling if not the dying of what has been. We have witnessed that truth played out in the march of civilizations, often violently. You can only answer for yourself as to its witness in portions of your life, spiritual and otherwise. In our journeys, some doors do need to be decisively closed and former ways permanently terminated if life is ever to take hold or new seeds are ever to germinate.

Seeds: Isaiah ends this bleak picture confronting Israel with a stark new image of God. When all seems hopeless, Isaiah says something about "the holy seed is its stump." The Hebrew text is so obscure and corrupt that the exact meaning of this phrase escapes conclusive determination. But perhaps that is always the nature of hope: We are not able to put our finger on it; we are not able to describe exactly or define what shape hope will take. But even in the most despairing of times—and words— a seed remains. Maybe Isaiah's seed is like those of pines, which require fire to release them from cones in order to germinate.

> *Do not abandon me, O God, but deliver me from all that would separate me from you, no matter how close or dear it may be. And even if much be required, grant me a seed to plant hope. Amen.*

SPIRITUAL EXERCISE

Read Isaiah 6:9-13. Focus upon an experience when your eyes and ears and mind missed some important piece of life or faith. In your journal, note what eventually brought you to "turning and healing." Reflect in like manner on how your community of faith "missed" an important piece and what eventually brought recognition. Prayerfully seek God's opening of your life today.

DAY 3

✦

When Word Comes

JEREMIAH 1:4-10

Now the word of the LORD came to me.—Jeremiah 1:4

I AM WAITING FOR some word." What setting or remembrance might that statement evoke in your mind? You may envision a hospital waiting room where family and friends gather in hope or fear of news yet to emerge from behind the closed doors of a delivery room or surgical wing. Or you might recall a time spent beside a phone, waiting for a call that would offer relief or confirm fears. When word finally comes in any such settings, life can change. Things may never be the same.

To Jeremiah and, through that prophet, to Israel came the word of God. The book that bears Jeremiah's name opens with a word that will make extraordinary claims and bring unprecedented upheaval to prophet and community. Jeremiah's cautionary protest on the basis of his youth rings understandable. His reluctance hints at just how intrusive this word will be within his life and that of his people. When this word comes, life will change. For Jeremiah and for Judah, things will never be the same.

Jeremiah describes this transformation with verbs that will become frequent companions in later visions of judgment: *pluck up, pull down, destroy, overthrow.* To a nation grown complacent in its sense of self-righteousness and entangled in foreign intrigues to save themselves, the word of God comes to sweep aside false hopes to make space for true hope.

Those same verbs play a role in the preparation to be made for spiritual reformation within persons. It is possible to construct all manner of assurances about our standing before God. Complacency can set in when we presume to know all we need to know about God. Arrogance can take root when we think we do all we need to do in response to God's purposes for us. Good works and spiritual disciplines cannot substitute for a living encounter with a word that insists on its control of our lives rather than the other way around.

Jeremiah proclaims the uncomfortable yet necessary word of that truth. Transformation and reformation come on God's terms. Faithfulness in the context of the message that comes to Jeremiah does not consist of duplicating what has been done in times past. Rather, faithfulness opens self and community wholeheartedly to the Holy One who puts words upon the lips and lives willing to trust God's transforming presence.

To be sure, not all is demand here. When this word comes—to Jeremiah, to us—there is also promise. "Do not be afraid . . . for I am with you." Those words may sound familiar, for they occur often in the biblical witness. They sound the promise made to Mary before incarnation. They reflect the assurance given to disciples on a storm-tossed and Jesus-walked sea. They come to the apostles (and through them to the church) at the conclusion of Matthew's Gospel.

"Do not be afraid . . . for I am with you." When you think about it, such words only bear promise to those who know fear or face isolation. For Jeremiah, this call preceded a vocation that would bring its share of both upon him. Yet when the word came, Jeremiah prophesied.

That word intends to transform you and me. At the beginning of such transformation comes the task of clearing aside whatever might stand in the way of making that word part of life. Jeremiah sought an out by stating, "I am only a youth" (RSV). We might substitute any number of things for "youth" that would hold us back—or that we would withhold from God's transformation. In those instances, we may need to hear the verbs of Jeremiah addressing us in a new way. Pulling up, breaking down, overthrowing, destroying, might be needed preparatory steps in our spiritual journey to make room for that which God would build up and plant.

When such a word comes, life may change. But the promise is this: No matter the change, we need not fear. God will be with us.

What word do you bring to me, O God: to speak, to enact, to re-form my life in your image and toward your calling? Your word has given me life. May your word continue to shape it. Amen.

SPIRITUAL EXERCISE

Reread Jeremiah 1:4-10. Listen in Jeremiah's responses to hesitations you may have voiced about some aspect of service or spiritual growth. In your journal, identify one set of misgivings you have now about a calling in your life. Name the difficulties and the questions. Then be at prayer about a word God might bring to you in this matter. Listen more than speak. Trust that a word will come. Return to this prayer as needed in coming days and weeks.

DAY 4

In the Potter's Hands

JEREMIAH 18:1-12

Can I not do with you . . . just as this potter
has done?—Jeremiah 18:6

A WET LUMP OF clay spins on a wheel. Hands shape it, form a depression within it, smooth it, round it . . . and then, it happens. An edge slumps. The whole piece goes out of balance. The wheel slows. The shape, now out of shape, finds itself pressed if not pounded back into a lump once more. Kneaded. Rolled. Molded. And then the process begins again.

A lump of clay may not express our highest conception of the human condition. Yet this passage is not the first time the biblical witness links our essence with the earth. "The LORD God formed man [*adam*] from the dust of the ground [*adamah*]" (Gen. 2:7). Those who take offense at the theory of human descent from primates may not have thought through the full import of our descent from such ooze as sticks to our boots on a walk through the marsh. "Earthenware" stamps who we are by God's fashioning of *adamah*.

Our earthen fashioning continues long after Genesis. Jeremiah receives direction to go to a potter's house, where word will be given in the allegory of God as potter and Israel as clay. "Out of [dust] you were taken . . . and to dust you shall return" (Gen.

3:19). This earthen bracketing of life and death is extended further in the parable. Humanity remains clay. That is the word Jeremiah—and we—find demonstrated at the potter's house.

Humanity as clay, in Jeremiah's context, is a word of judgment. It doesn't need to be, mind you. The allegory itself drives home the point that clay in the hand of a potter need not be an image to fear or despise or avoid. The potter brings to this word the possibility of creative opportunity. A mere lump of clay can become art or a vessel that sustains or enriches life.

The note of judgment in this image of humanity as clay and God as potter, for Israel and perhaps for us, resounds in God's freedom to reshape the clay as God chooses. Persons and communities tend to become accustomed to the "shape" they have taken over the years. Traditions can (not *must* but *can*) become rigid. Attitudes can harden. Preferences and opinions can become redefined into norms and canons. Deviations from popular perceptions or conventional wisdom can be met with inflexible denial. When clay ceases to be pliable and malleable, it cannot be worked on the potter's wheel.

The twelfth verse gives voice to the rigid inflexibility of the community whom Jeremiah addressed. "It is no use! We will follow our own plans." Not even God can bear to look at the consequences of their intransigence: "I will show them my back, not my face" (Jer. 18:17).

A comic strip named *Pogo* once declared, "We have met the enemy, and he is us." In Jeremiah, resistance to change and transformation makes Israel its own worse enemy. How often have God's purposes to rework our lives been thwarted by heels dug in, minds set, or spirits closed? Jeremiah wrote to such a community. His words continue to speak with poignance and power to groups and individuals who will have nothing to do with changing direction or reforming old ways.

But Jeremiah's words also speak to individuals who, for whatever reason, balk at having their lives reworked. Comfort with how things are, a desire to control whatever might come to be, fear of the new or untried: Feel free to jump in here and add your own objections to being placed on the potter's wheel.

God's freedom to rework persons and communities generates both the offense and the hope in this word given to Jeremiah at the potter's house. Verse 12 reports the response of a community unwilling to trust itself at that one moment into such reforming. But the text need not lead to that. Reworking the clay into another vessel seemed good to the potter. Does God's reworking of the clay that is your life seem good to you?

> *Soften me to your touch, Creator God. Fashion me, rework me, as seems good to you. And in the midst of such change and even stress, may I find it good as well. In Jesus Christ. Amen.*

SPIRITUAL EXERCISE

Find modeling clay or some other moldable medium. Work it in your hands while you read Jeremiah 18:1-4. Continue working it while you reflect on an experience in your life when you sensed God "reworking" who you were. As you continue working the clay, open yourself in prayer to how God may be reshaping your life even now. Offer thanks and seek patience for that reworking.

DAY 5

✦

How Do You View God?

EZEKIEL 1:4-28

The heavens were opened, and I saw visions of God.—Ezekiel 1:1

IF YOU ARE like me, this question may send you scurrying to read how others have seen God. The Christian community is, after all, a people of the Book. You might very likely frame your first response based on what has been said of God in authoritative places and authoritative ways. And there is nothing wrong with that except—except if all your thoughts on that subject come from times and experiences not your own. There is nothing wrong except when such ideas become so predictable and domesticated they are less passionate testimony and more disinterested recitation or partisan rhetoric. No one could accuse Ezekiel of a domesticated view of God. The vision he relates in the "throne-chariot vision" of chapter 1 is anything but tame. God takes shape there in storm winds and bright cloud and lightning flash. Four living creatures, each with four faces, wheels within wheels that hold the spirit of the living creatures, reveal Deity. Tell your Wednesday afternoon Bible study group that you had this vision of God the other night and watch the reactions.

Nor could Ezekiel be charged with a predictable view of God. While individual elements of his vision find precedents in Jewish and Near Eastern imagery, Ezekiel wraps his package of God's likeness in ways distinct from anyone before or since. In contrast, popular piety and wider society prefer to depict God in the mantle of unchanging character. "We blossom and flourish as leaves on the tree, and wither and perish, but naught changeth thee" ("Immortal, Invisible, God Only Wise"). "Jesus Christ is the same yesterday and today and forever" (Heb. 13:8). If nothing else can be depended upon, we can trust God's remaining constant. Right?

Well, there are other notes that make the biblical witness a harmony rather than a monotone when the subject turns to God's (un)predictability. Abraham bargains with God for the fate of Sodom, securing an increasingly smaller number of righteous as the baseline for sparing the city (Gen. 18:22-33). Moses intercedes with God to spare a disobedient Israel, "and the LORD changed his mind about the disaster that he planned to bring on his people" (Exod. 32:11-14). New circumstances can bring fresh responses, even from God. God's adaptation to such intercession bears witness to the dynamic nature of God's freedom to act in gracious and even surprising ways.

Theorists can argue until the end of history as to whether such "change" falls more on the side of God's unpredictability or our lack of perception. Ezekiel does not engage in such speculative conversation. Ezekiel simply yet profoundly confronts Israel with a revisioning of God to meet the crisis of that moment. Routine ways of perceiving God would not adequately address a people in need of a new—and probably unwelcome—vision of a God free to move beyond the confines of tradition.

Ezekiel bears this same witness of God to persons and communities of faith today. How do we view God? If we take Ezekiel to heart, we may find those views subject to change and revision. The God envisioned by Ezekiel may not always take familiar paths. The God envisioned by Ezekiel is anything but immobile, either in terms of where God goes or where God summons us to follow. The God who seeks our transformation may speak through fresh sources and unexpected places if we have become too comfortable in the routine of our spirituality. Like Ezekiel, the God who invites us and beckons our communities to renewal is a God of wheels, a God of movement and freedom—and hope for new life.

> *Grant me eyes to see your coming and working in ways new as well as old. Grant me faith to follow where you go today. Grant me grace to serve you in the unfolding of this new day. Amen.*

SPIRITUAL EXERCISE

Reflect on a time when you found your ideas about God stretched or challenged. In your journal, note what created that invitation to revisit and revision God. Consider how that experience has shaped not simply your beliefs about God but your participation in community and the hopes that motivate your service. Be in prayer about new invitations or challenges to your faith.

DAY 6

✦

The Unboxed God

EZEKIEL 10:9-22; 11:22-25

*Then the glory of the LORD went out from the
threshold of the house.—Ezekiel 10:18*

I AM, I CONFESS, into control. I enjoy it when life is ordered and, even more importantly, dependable. I prefer having matters wrapped into neat packages that will unfold as planned. Ask my wife. She will recall summer vacations that entered the preparation stage the previous fall.

In contrast, modern physics argues that the smallest elements of matter are in a state of constant motion and flux. What appears to be solid, be it a table or your own body, is actually a wildly vibrating collection of material. Were it not for strange forces at work within atoms, the illusion of solidity would scatter into nothingness. I try not to lose sleep over being poised on the edge of such a precipice. I prefer dependability, even if it be mere appearance. How else could I live?

I do not count myself alone on that matter, and I am not speaking of modern physics solely. When it comes to religion—whether in the heart of an individual or the spirit of a community—we largely prefer to live in comfort zones constructed of what we have come to depend upon in our belief systems. I have observed that behavior to hold true whether one falls into the camp of rabid conservatives or flaming liberals or any faith position in between. How did we get this way? Our experiences have taught us. Our traditions have presented us a base to accept or a plank to reject. Our encounters with God have shaped us. We package our faith in a way that makes sense and works according to our thinking. How else could we live?

There is only one slight problem with this tendency: God. God's quicksilver-like resistance to being poured into one shape or confined into one box eludes our control. Just when we think we have this faith thing nailed down and dependable, God goes contrarian.

Ask the folks addressed by Ezekiel. Everybody *knew* God dwelt in the Jerusalem Temple. That was the covenant; that was the agreement. God would stay put no matter what. Jerusalem would be secure no matter what. You could always count on that truth if nothing else. But when the "nothing else" of exile came to pass, lo and behold, God didn't stay put. God moved beyond not just expectations but beyond the Temple door, beyond the city gate, beyond the Promised Land. God had wheels, and God was in motion "straight ahead." Straight to the future.

Israel may not have known about particle physics and chaos theories, but through Ezekiel Israel came to know that things are not always what they appear. Israel discovered something far more unsettling than a table not as solid as it seems: The box they had constructed for God could not restrain deity. A religious system based on a resident and therefore status-quo–assuring Presence proved an illusion. Israel confronted a new reality when Ezekiel described God's Presence leaving the holy city.

God's freedom was—and remains—a sobering sight. All our constructions (or are they constrictions?) of God, whether liturgical, theological, social, or "spiritual formational," at best only bear witness to the living God. We catch a glimpse; we receive a promise; we partake a grace; we hear a challenge. If we think we have God figured out or under lock and key, wheels start spinning and wings start flapping. God proves elusive to every attempt at boxing in to a favored tradition or position.

To encounter this God and to be formed by that encounter summon acknowledgment of God's freedom. That freedom hedges every human attempt to coerce God's power, presume upon God's favor, or limit God's full reality to our partial understandings.

Ezekiel witnesses to God's freedom not as capriciousness, though, but as purposeful and ultimately hopeful. When God leaves Jerusalem, the Presence moves east: the direction of the exiles, the direction of Israel's future. God's freedom does not move God to abandon us. God's freedom moves God to find us, to lead us to places we have never known—and perhaps might never have gone—had it not been for the God too large for any box to contain. Ezekiel's God has wheels and wings!

As I would dwell in your Light, O God, remind me that dwelling is better served by a tent that can be packed and moved in order to keep up with you. Amen.

SPIRITUAL EXERCISE

Imagine God with wings and wheels, free to move when and where needed. Reread this session's texts from Ezekiel. In your journal, reflect on where God might be moving out ahead of you at this moment in your spiritual journey and in the ministry of your church. Pray for wisdom and discernment in understanding how God's freedom may be at work in your life and congregation now, bidding you (and others) to follow in new ways.

WEEK TWO

CASTING OFF ILLUSIONS

DAY I

Superficials and Essentials

ISAIAH 1:10-20

When you come to appear before me, who asked this from your hand?—Isaiah 1:12

YEARS AGO I took a creative writing course when I first explored the idea of combining pastoral ministry with a ministry exercised through the written word. Early on in that class, the question of how one makes time and space for writing arose. After all, nearly everyone in the class either had a current vocation or active retirement that routinely swallowed the hours of the days. The leader responded to the question with a graphic though difficult solution: Take a broadax to your schedule. In other words, cut away the nonessentials. Hack away activities that may have been important or needed once but that now have become secondary. Prune back whatever simply takes time without really contributing to your life or the lives of others. And in those spaces, write. A writer is one who does not merely think about writing, read books about writing, or take courses about writing. A writer is one who writes.

Writing and a vital spiritual life require the same discipline. Trim away the superficialities. Get to the heart of the matter, the essentials. Do what needs to be done.

Isaiah 1:10-20 originally addressed individuals and a society whose religious practices had become superficial. The actions vilified in these verses were not in themselves without merit or significance. Search the Hebrew scripture and rabbinic teachings. You will find ample justification for all these matters Isaiah called into question: the place of offerings, the observance of seasonal celebrations, the lifting of prayers. The problem arose elsewhere. "I cannot endure solemn assemblies with iniquity. . . . Even though you make many prayers, I will not listen; your hands are full of blood" (vv. 13, 15). A gap existed between liturgy and living. Inattention to the essentials of doing good and seeking justice made superficial these otherwise valid expressions of piety. Isaiah addressed attitudes and practices that lulled Israel's walk with God into the equivalent of sleepwalking. Habits and rituals had become habitual and ritualistic, separated from the wider life intended to be transformed by these disciplines.

As did my mentor in writing, Isaiah offers a "broadax" solution. He confronts Israel's spiritual crisis with a series of imperative verbs. Wash; make yourselves clean; remove the evil; cease to do evil; learn to do good; seek justice; rescue; defend; plead. In other words, hack away the cosmetic accretions that cover over and swallow up what is essential in the journey with God. Go to the heart of the matter. Do what needs to be done.

Spiritual growth and formation today involve that same discipline. For some, the crunch may come in settings and issues quite similar to Isaiah's context. Public worship can still ignore the public good. Devotional practices can still be observed in utter obliviousness to one's business or social practices. Through the words of Isaiah, not to mention Jesus, we gain a sharper insight into the need for individuals and communities to keep such matters close to heart.

Spiritual formation involves peeling away the superficial in order to target the essentials. For example, we may immerse ourselves in the mechanics of religious institutions to the point of losing sight of why we do what we do. The busy-ness of board meetings and institutional maintenance may neglect the inner compass that develops through intimate relationship with God. We need continual reorientation to what is truly needful, not only for our personal spiritual journey but for seeking what is good and just for our neighbor.

Isaiah voices hard words, but necessary ones, to keep in perspective what is essential to relationship with God. Spiritual formation invokes that same effort on your part. It invites you to strip away the accumulation of practices and assumptions that substitute themselves for genuine encounters with God. Spiritual formation seeks, if I may paraphrase my writing instructor, one who does not merely read about formation or talk about formation or take classes in formation. Spiritual formation pries you open to the Spirit's re-forming of your life, pruning what has become superficial in your walk with God in order to uncover what remains essential.

Trouble me, O God, when I am content with the superficial: in vocation, in community, in faith. Immerse me in that which is essential: for good, for truth, for life. Amen.

SPIRITUAL EXERCISE

Read Isaiah 1:10-20 aloud. If Isaiah had addressed this text to you or to your congregation, imagine what he might have substituted for "bringing offerings" or "festivals" as activities that have become superficial. What essentials would he admonish you and your community to recover? Seek God's guidance in prayer for ways you might bring these essentials to the fore in your life and in your community.

DAY 2

Stumps

ISAIAH 11:1-5

A shoot shall come out from the stump of Jesse.—Isaiah 11:1

THE SOUTH END of Sullivan Lake in Pend Oreille County, Washington, can produce a remarkable sight. When the water level falls enough to expose the old delta created by Harvey Creek (now usually flooded because the lake's north end is dammed), a huge stretch of stumps comes into view. The stumps are enormous. One can only imagine the forest that once stood there, apparently logged just before the lake was artificially raised. But when the water drops, those grey stumps are revealed with no sign of life.

"A shoot shall come out from the stump of Jesse." Those words cannot be understood apart from the close of chapter 10, where Isaiah declares God's intent to engage in "clear-cutting" no less drastic in its effects than what happened to the old delta of Harvey Creek. It takes nerve to recognize, much less call, Israel's dynastic line a wad of decaying wood fiber that no longer has any life of its own. It takes a great act of courage to confess what has grown old and tired in one's own life or within one's community. But before Isaiah's promise can be seen, judgment must be admitted. It all begins with a stump.

Reforming spiritual vitality at times requires such honesty and courage to name what is vital and what is dead among us. The easier path lies in resting on laurels or replaying the fire of past experiences and institutions whose times have come and gone. Isaiah confronted a community grown smug in the security of chosenness. Israel lulled itself into presuming life as God's elect bestowed a guarantee of status quo rather than a calling to keep covenant. In such a context, even promise can pronounce judgment. If life is ever to emerge from lifeless stumps, it will be on God's terms.

In the area where I now live, old-growth stumps quickly become overgrown by brush and berry, then alder and evergreen. Some stumps eventually serve as nursery platforms for another generation of bushes and trees. How does that happen? The old, dead wood in the stump's core softens and breaks apart sufficiently for a seed to send down roots and find nourishment. In some cases, the tree growing from that stump wraps its roots around the outside of the stump, using it as anchor before it finally establishes those roots in the ground.

Some parts of our lives in need of dying or setting aside can serve a similar function of providing a platform for fresh growth. We can plant new disciplines that take root in the "stump" of worn devotional practice or personal behavior. Such planting and rooting requires softening those former places, opening lives and communities to new seeds and tender roots. If we encase those former things in unyielding traditions or bitterness about what is no longer, we guarantee nothing new will come. The inner life of persons or communities can form hardened patches that resemble those stumps at Sullivan Lake: remarkable witnesses to what once was but without any life now. Stumps can remain just stumps. For some in ancient Israel, inability to move beyond the past and unwillingness to confront realities of the present left them unable to see God's purposes. They could not see that judgment neared. They could not accept the promise of hope built on a stump.

The transformative element in this passage, whether applied to eighth-century BCE Israel or to persons seeking spiritual reformation in the twenty-first century CE, is God's Spirit. The Spirit of God defines the character of the one promised as Messiah—and more. The Spirit of God enables persons and communities today to trust in God's re-creative and re-formative purposes. Stumps do not sport growth by accident. Judgment does not yield to hope by chance. Persons do not re-form their spiritual lives in a vacuum. Creation and re-creation occur when God's Spirit moves to bring life out of dead places. Isaiah saw Israel's hope as a community in that reality. Through Isaiah, we recognize that possibility in our spiritual journeys as well.

"A shoot shall come out from the stump." From judgment comes hope; from death comes life. Isaiah's stump breaks ground for Jesus' Cross.

> *Sow seeds in my faith where new growth may spring from old. Soften my spirit to your Spirit's working and planting. And where I am in need of dying, bring fresh life. In Jesus Christ. Amen.*

SPIRITUAL EXERCISE

Read Isaiah 11:1 aloud. Envision where you have experienced new growth taking root on old "stumps" in your spiritual journey. Offer a prayer of thanks for new growth that has come in times past and for openness to opportunities when it might yet emerge unexpectedly.

DAY 3

✦

Deceptive Words

JEREMIAH 7:1-15

Do not trust in these deceptive words.—Jeremiah 7:4

IN JUNE OF 1972 I attended Explo '72 in Dallas, Texas, along with tens of thousands of other young persons. The week-long event blended training seminars, opportunities for witness, and gatherings for worship. Every night we filled the Cotton Bowl for singing and preaching focused on a designated theme. On God and Country evening—this was Dallas; the year was 1972; and Vietnam was still a very hot war and a very divisive topic—something memorable happened. As a procession of flags was borne into the stadium, a small group at the far corner of the stadium began to chant, "Stop the war!" I don't think more than a couple of dozen voices raised that cry, but it was unmistakable. Then, in reply, came a few, and then more, and finally thousands of other voices, going, "Sssssssshhhhh" until the protesters could no longer be heard.

That night in the Cotton Bowl, an unwelcome word was "shushed" by folks whose focus on worship excluded some stark and painful realities outside our "sanctuary."

Likewise Jeremiah stepped up to a Temple gate where a large throng of worshipers approached. Residents of Jerusalem joined with pilgrims from all over Judah. Together they journeyed to the Holy Sanctuary where God dwells, the place whose very existence guaranteed the city's and the nation's security. Instead of leading the people in a good old-time hymn, the preacher sounded a sour note. "Amend your ways and your doings." And he didn't stop there. Twice Jeremiah berated the people for trusting in deceptive words. Some commentators believe the people attempted to drown out this bearer of bad news with the chant: "This is the temple of the LORD, the temple of the LORD, the temple of the LORD." It was the equivalent of the Cotton Bowl's "Sssshhhhhhh!"

According to Jeremiah, those were the deceptive words. The deception consisted of trusting a static place instead of a dynamic covenant. Places, even holy places invested with generations of religious memories, cannot substitute for acting justly, for showing compassion to the vulnerable, for remaining faithful to the Holy One of Israel. The prophet's reference to Shiloh in verse 12 as presaging what may come to Judah teemed with irony. Psalm 78:60-69 had contrasted God's rejection of Shiloh with God's love for Mount Zion and its sanctuary. "Do not trust in these deceptive words" (v. 4).

The problem is deceptive words need not be bad words. Deceptive beliefs need not be bad beliefs. The Temple represented a place of sacred encounter where people believed the very presence of God dwelled. In and of itself, that idea was not wrong. It became misleading only when folks presumed that the reliability of covenant with God allowed them to ignore the demands of that covenant. As a result, hopes shifted from dynamic covenantal relationship with God to illusions provided by static institutions. "This is the temple of the LORD. . . ."

What deceives people today with illusory hope? Specific answers to match every reader's situation surpass the limits of this book. But if Jeremiah can be trusted, look for deception where people say something like, "I know all I need to know."

Look where gaps exist between liturgical practice and daily living. Look where language of God glosses over how people are treated, paid, kept in line, or stereotyped. Look where God always seems to be declared as one of us and on our side. And do not be afraid to look within as well as without. Sometimes we can be all too keen at detecting the deceptions snaring others and oblivious to our own peculiar gullibility.

The seduction of deceptive words lies in their attractiveness. They confirm what we want to believe or assume. They leave us alone in our frailties and prejudice. They excuse us from difficult responsibilities. They go, "Sssssshhhh," when we need to start into wakefulness. Deception is at its most alluring when it comes couched in the guise of what we hold to be good. Temple, patriotism, church polity: Whatever tickles our ears with the promise that this is *really* what it's all about deceives. For if Jeremiah rightly speaks the word God gives, the test of such claims comes in justice done, in mercy extended, and in loyalty to God.

> *Restore me, O God, to trust rooted in you. And may the way I live be consistent with and faithful to your purposes for justice and mercy and holiness. In Jesus Christ. Amen.*

SPIRITUAL EXERCISE

In your journal, list the "deceptions" you see at work today: in the lives of individuals, in the church, in your wider community and society. Reread Jeremiah 7:1-15. Mark one of the deceptions that you find particularly difficult in your life. Mark another of the deceptions that seems to be a real issue in your church. Mark another that holds powerful sway in the community in which you live. Reread verses 5–6. Reflect on how Jeremiah's words speak to each of those issues. Pray for guidance in confronting such deception.

DAY 4

✦

The Myth of Fairness

JEREMIAH 12:1-6

Why does the way of the guilty prosper?—Jeremiah 12:1

IT IS A PAINFUL lesson for a child to learn and for a parent to interpret. Something dramatically unfair happens. A friend suffers. A parent leaves. A grandparent dies. Without any guile on her part, without any blame to be cast her way, the child wonders why such a thing must happen and why it must affect her so. We instruct our children in what is right. We teach the balance of actions and consequences. But what happens when the balance goes lopsided? When unfairness creeps into the equation of how things often work in this world?

Jeremiah faced a hard task and harsher reactions in his call to ministry and its results. Jeremiah 11:18-20 laments the scheming of those who seek Jeremiah's death in response to his prophesying. God follows the prophet's lament with a promise to bring disaster upon those who would silence him.

Such support, however, does not salve a deeper uneasiness in Jeremiah. Our verses begin with the prophet's willingness to address God. Actually, the more proper verb would be Jeremiah's readiness to *accuse* God. The accusation takes the form of a question: "Why does the way of the guilty prosper?" In other words, why is life not fair? Psalm 1 affirms the righteous will prosper while the wicked will perish. If that is so, laments

Jeremiah, "Why do all who are treacherous thrive?" The prophet becomes even more blunt: "You plant them, and they take root." God has a hand in their planting. Is that fair?

Jeremiah, like Job, presses God with the righteousness of his cause. Going beyond the scope of Job's complaint, he even pleads for the land itself, for a creation that withers under the effect of the wicked. Is that destruction fair? God's response to Jeremiah raises more questions than it answers, much as God brushed aside Job's case with the mystery of God's unfathomable ways. If things seem tough and unfair now, the message went, how will you fare in coming circumstances that will be far more severe? Fairness does not hold center stage in life. Faithfulness does: faithfulness that endures severe crisis, faithfulness that asserts a radical trust in God. The treachery of Jeremiah's family, described in the final verses, implies that the prophet has no one utterly dependable save God.

This radical trust in God in a world with no guarantee of fairness is revealed as a discipline of spiritual formation in this text. Please take note: The text does not loose us from the obligation to seek fairness for persons and community. God does not side with those who have intended Jeremiah violence. God does not enjoy the injustice that Jeremiah and others identify as the cause of impending judgment. No, what God communicates to Jeremiah in these verses is: Trust in me. Even if things get worse before they get better, even if voices much more tangible speak of other ways and other trusts, even if life does not seem to be fair or congruent, trust in me.

What God proposes to Jeremiah is no easy thing. It is no easy thing to trust in One confessed to be Holy when the unholy holds sway. It is no easy thing to trust in One confessed to be Love when unloving actions abound. It is no easy thing to trust in One confessed to be Just when unfairness rears its head in costly and painful ways.

For these reasons, Jeremiah 12 may seem odd reading when life flows in pleasant ways. It may not make sense when life makes utmost sense. Then again, Jeremiah may be the very prophet needed for sedated spirits in docile times. Why? Ease and fairness will not always go unchallenged in your life and the lives of those around you. When events turn unfair, when the guilty prosper, when an innocent of any age turns to you in tears at some outrage inflicted, you will need Jeremiah. You will need Jeremiah, as will I, to remember what is not promised in life and what is. Fairness is not. God is.

"You will be in the right, O LORD, when I lay charges against you; but let me put my case to you." Jeremiah will not let go of God, even when fairness is nowhere to be found. Nor will Jeremiah bury his questions about God's hand and purposes in a creation that suffers on account of evil. Jeremiah invites us to such prayer. God invites us to such trust.

> *God, I also wonder why the guilty prosper. I too question the unfairness of life. But in my wonder and in my questions, O God, hold me to your call so I will not stumble when greater challenges await. Hold me in trust that does not let go of you, come what may. Amen.*

SPIRITUAL EXERCISE

In your journal, reflect on a specific incident of unfairness in which you found your faith or sense of vocation tested. Reread Jeremiah 12:5. Consider a conflict facing the community in which you live or your congregation. How do the challenges in that situation compare to larger issues abroad? Be at prayer about ways you and your congregation or community might faithfully address that situation.

DAY 5

A Failure to Communicate

EZEKIEL 3:4-11
---

*But the house of Israel will not listen to you, for they are
not willing to listen to me.—Ezekiel 3:7*

IN THE MOVIE *Cool Hand Luke,* a prison farm warden admonishes his rebellious prisoner, Luke, before the entire camp. "What we've got here is failure to communicate," he declares to explain why drastic punishment will be required. Near the end of the movie, searchers and bloodhounds surround an old building where runaway Luke and a compatriot have taken refuge. Luke cannot resist one final shouted protest to the assembled posse as to what has brought them all to this place: "What we got here is a failure to communicate." He barely gets out the words before a bullet brings death.

Death and communication failures do not limit themselves to movie screenplays. Husbands and wives over the course of years find themselves unable or unwilling to speak civil, much less loving, words. Relationships die. Parents and children talk past rather than to one another. Trust dies. Nations or religions in conflict settle for words that simply spout slogans or espouse positions, never bending to listen or empathize. Peace dies.

Failures in communication can be traced to different languages spoken by antagonists. The biblical story of Babel puts a sharp edge on problems generated by variant tongues that divide and confuse us. If that story seems too remote, read a technical journal written in a field in which you have little or no experience. Babel is not so far away as it seems.

Inaccessible language can pose enormous difficulties for understanding. On the other hand, a common language does not guarantee unanimity. God dispatches Ezekiel to the house of Israel to "speak my very words to them." One might think the problem would be getting the words right. Wrong. The real problem will be getting the words listened to: not accepted but just heard. You can tell all the truth you want, but if no one listens, communication breaks down.

This passage in Ezekiel sets aside the deception that communication rests entirely on the shoulders of one person or one side of the equation. Ezekiel receives the God-given commission "to speak my very words" not to force Israel to comply. God liberates Ezekiel from having to guarantee the outcome, which might result in the prophet's unconscious desire to shape or twist or "smooth over" that word to make it more palatable. What people do with that word, God suggests, is not Ezekiel's burden. Whether they hear or refuse to hear makes no difference in terms of the commission. Whether Israel hears or refuses to hear becomes Israel's responsibility. From Ezekiel God seeks only a clear communication of that word. And let the chips fall where they may.

To be spiritually formed by this text may take you in several directions. One, from the example of the prophet, comes in the freedom to speak and enact the word God brings unfettered by the need to please or convince everyone. This can be an exacting discipline if you are, as I am, one whose inclination tends toward not rocking boats and toward solving everyone's problems. Ezekiel could not listen on behalf of Israel and certainly could not decide and do what God sought of Israel. "Say to them, 'Thus says the LORD God'; whether they hear or refuse to hear." Speak the word and trust God to accomplish what may come of it or not. God offers sage advice then and now.

We see another aspect of spiritual formation from this text in the example of Israel. Communication requires a partner. The words of God need engagement of ears, hearts, and wills if that word will ever be heard and enacted. In Ezekiel's time, judgment resulted because of a failure to listen.

"You are not sent to a people of obscure speech and difficult language." Sometimes the most difficult tasks in communicating lie in speaking and listening to those closest to home. From Ezekiel learn to speak, learn to listen—and learn to (en)trust the results to God.

> *Tune my ear to hear, and my mouth to speak, and my life*
> *to live the Word you bring to me in Jesus Christ. Amen.*

SPIRITUAL EXERCISE

Reread Ezekiel 3:4-11. In your journal, reflect on some situation in which you have found yourself in Ezekiel's place, called to speak a word people did not heed. What sustained you? Consider "words" that your community or congregation currently has difficulty listening to these days. What creates those difficulties? Be at prayer for the community's and your own openness to words God might be waiting to be heard.

DAY 6

✦

Clockmaker No Longer

EZEKIEL 12:21-28

*It will no longer be delayed . . . I will speak the word and
fulfill it, says the Lord GOD.—Ezekiel 12:25*

IN THE SEVENTEENTH and eighteenth centuries, the Enlightenment dominated western European thought with its
emphasis upon rationalism and scientific method. Reason
rather than revelation became the chief means by which
human beings understood the world around them. Such ideas
about nature spilled into the realm of theology. One popular-
ized tenet of this movement invoked the image of God as a
great divine clockmaker. In this image, God crafted the laws
and realities of nature and then basically stepped out of the
way to watch it all run in its inherent beauty and symmetry.
Rationalism rejected the supernatural and therefore the intervention of God in history or the natural processes.

On the surface few parallels seem likely between belea-
guered Israelites confronting exile (whom Ezekiel addressed)
and the deists of emerging modern western philosophy. But
on the point of God's absence or withdrawal from the world,
these two groups agreed. Ezekiel's audience may not have had
the Enlightenment's imagery of "clockmaker," but they did
share the conviction that God was a nonplayer.

"'The days are prolonged, and every vision comes to nothing.' . . . 'The vision that he sees is for many years ahead; he prophesies for distant times.'" These two "proverbs" Ezekiel records suggest the practical implications of God's apparent withdrawal. As prophet he faces people with an attitude that might be summed up: *If God is nowhere to be seen except on the far horizon, why bother? Why listen to visions, particularly those of judgment that we do not want to hear anyway?* God can be put off. The attitude bears disturbing resemblance to those inane bumper stickers one sometimes sees today on luxury vehicles: "We're spending our children's inheritance." Disregard for the future inevitably poisons the present.

God responds to those who relegate God to distant corners of the universe and remote moments of the future: *I am here.* The future is now. What may have been forbearance to allow time for change to emerge becomes an hourglass whose sands have all plummeted to the bottom. "'I will put an end to this proverb.' . . . None of my words will be delayed any longer." God will no longer be the detached and disinterested clockmaker, as if God ever had been that passive observer. Passion, not passivity, marks the Holy One who parted waters and delivered slaves and put Pharaoh to shame. Passion, not passivity, marks the Sovereign One who refuses to be dismissed as irrelevant or put off by those who have forgotten the old stories and thus have forgotten God's power.

The illusion of God's distance and disinterest continues to delude those of us who prefer not to be bothered by this God's visions, which complicate our lives as individuals and communities. Were God to stay out of the way, we could do things more efficiently without compassion and justice to clutter the way. Were God to stay out of the way, we could allow personal opinions, not to mention prejudices, to dictate what courses we follow. Were God to stay out of the way, we could avoid taking hard looks inside our spirits and inside our institutions or seeking the even harder change therein.

"The word that I speak will be fulfilled." Spiritual formation in the light of Ezekiel requires taking those words and that fulfillment seriously. I do not mean "serious" as in long faces and dour spirits. Indeed, to acknowledge God's active presence evokes joy and hope not often accessible in a world grimly insisting all things must be as they always have been. Rather, I invoke *serious* as synonym for *real*: trust-worthy. To be spiritually formed by this text invites us to live with the freedom and hope to trust God's purposes will not go denied.

"The word that I speak will be fulfilled." In the immediate context of Ezekiel 12, that word sounded judgment. It still may today. But it also may engender hope and encourage discipleship. Disinterested Clockmaker or Passionate Advocate: Our lives reveal which image of God we choose to follow.

> *Holy God, Sovereign Christ, Free-Moving Spirit: Renew me in trust and in hope and in a steadfast seeking of that which you promise. For in you would I trust. Amen.*

SPIRITUAL EXERCISE

Reread Ezekiel 12:21-28. What "visions" test the patience of faith today or create cynicism about promises too distant, too removed, too hard, for these times? Be at prayer for fresh actions that may renew hope and trust and faithful action. Talk with another person who shares similar outlooks and seek to find ways of encouraging one another and renewing your community.

WEEK THREE

Speaking Truth to Power

DAY 1

✦

Wearying God

ISAIAH 7:1-17

Is it too little for you to weary mortals, that you
weary my God also?—Isaiah 7:13

How could you tire out God? Some might appeal to the first chapter of Genesis, where six "days" of creation's labors moved God to rest. However, Genesis 1 makes no mention of weariness as the root of sabbath. Others might suggest Jacob's wrestling with a stranger—often interpreted to be God—at Peniel (Gen. 32:22-32). But even there the stranger seeks release not in connection with weariness but with the approach of day.

So how can you be guaranteed to weary God? If you believe Isaiah 7, live as though God makes no difference. Refuse to trust God in times of risk. Let fear dictate your choices.

Isaiah's narrative concerns a particular episode in the reign of King Ahaz. Confronted with news of a political and military menace posed by two hostile neighboring kings, "the heart of Ahaz and the heart of his people shook as the trees of the forest shake before the wind." Fear can move palpably among us. Fear can overwhelm us with the threat of death, of failure, of dismissal, of disfavor. You don't have to be a king to understand, to experience, fear.

God directs Isaiah to speak to Ahaz. The message intended does not offer pity but empowerment. God declares to Ahaz through Isaiah that this menace and the fear it generates does not have staying power. Finally, God makes clear what Ahaz must do and the consequences for failure: "If you do not stand firm in faith, you shall not stand at all."

Stand firm. Faith here does not come revealed in intellectual assent to doctrinal propositions nor in emotional fervor. Faith involves standing firm in the face of fear. Faith trusts in God's purposes rather than insisting on self-reliance.

In an act of extraordinary grace, God invites Ahaz to ask a sign, an indication that God can be trusted. Ahaz faces a choice: *Live by faith*, trusting God to stand firm in the face of a siege against Jerusalem by the northern kingdom of Israel and Syria, or *live by fear*, trusting an alliance with treacherous Assyria to survive. Political expedience rather than radical trust wins the day. Ahaz even alludes to scripture in order to keep God at bay: "I will not put the LORD to the test" (see Deut. 6:16). To which Isaiah replies: "Is it too little for you to weary mortals, that you weary my God also?" There you have the answer to how God can be wearied: Employ superficial piety as the excuse to dwell in fear and maintain personal control rather than risk deep trust in God.

The spirituality of Ahaz has much appeal. It allows us to leave God out of the messy practicalities of political affairs. Isaiah's message aimed to deter Ahaz from his realpolitik solution to the menace: alliance with Assyria. The spirituality of Ahaz allows us to hunker down in those scriptures that buoy our plans and ignore those that probe us. Ahaz could have remembered Psalm 33:16-17: "A king is not saved by his great army; . . . The war horse is a vain hope for victory." To do so, however, would have meant rethinking fond dreams of recruiting all those Assyrian troopers and chariots to *his* side.

To speak of the spirituality of Ahaz might seem an oxymoron, but in truth his spirituality forms the chief rival to the spirituality of Isaiah. With Ahaz, fear exorcises the need for trust. Fear eliminates the need for God, except as a popular icon to be trotted out for display. With Isaiah, trust exorcises the seductiveness of fear. Trust roots our lives wholly in God, especially when risks run high and choices turn costly.

Trust, like love, casts out fear—not by saying the threats are not there but by insisting God is also there. With God come alternatives. Ahaz refused the offer of a sign to reveal that alternative and so wearied God. We need not repeat the error. The sign Isaiah offered came in Immanuel, a word and child whose name promised "God is with us." We bear that sign in our trust of God who has come to us in Jesus Christ. We bear that sign in faith that trusts God in the face of contradicting claims about the source of security and peace.

When fear looms large, remember God's words to Isaiah, "Take heed, be quiet, do not fear and do not let your heart be faint . . . stand firm in faith."

> *Forgive me, O God, when I have wearied you—by lack of trust, by emptiness of love. Renew me. Strengthen me. Encourage me. For I would trust, and I would love, in you. Amen.*

SPIRITUAL EXERCISE

Read the final line in today's meditation above, the five imperatives God speaks through Isaiah. Offer each one as if it were a prayer Isaiah raises for you. In your journal, record your insights. That is, what do you need to heed? Where do you need quieting? What fears do you need to release? What makes you faint in heart? Where do you need to stand firm? Pray for God's help and strength as you ponder these questions.

DAY 2

Remnants

ISAIAH 10:20-23

A remnant will return.—Isaiah 10:21

IN THE NASELLE Congregational United Church of Christ a group of women gather twice a week to weave rugs. They arrange multiple strands of strong thread on the loom to form the warp. Through those threads they will pass a shuttle, which carries material called the weft (or woof) to make the weave that fashions the rug. To this point they do nothing out of the ordinary. What makes their creations unique is the material used for the weft. Instead of new threads of wool or unused skeins of yarn, they use strips of cut-up rags: remnants of discarded dresses, slacks, coats, robes, and who knows what else.

Looking at the piles of rags in the rug room waiting to be cut and rolled, it is hard to imagine anything useful, much less attractive, coming out of such clutter. Yet the rugs these women weave from rags and remnants are prized throughout the lower Columbia region of Washington state.

I have sometimes wondered if anyone looking at one of those rugs ever recognizes in the weave a favorite shirt or a much beloved dress. What would the person's reaction be? Would someone long for what had been but now never more would be? Would a sense of loss flow from remembering that piece of apparel being given by a friend or associated with a poignant moment in life? After all, remnants are just that, fragments of a now-lost whole.

Remnant looms large in this day's reading from Isaiah. The prophet invokes this term four times. Read the text through, and you will likely come away with mixed messages as to whether these words about remnants pronounce judgment or announce hope. Perhaps Isaiah intended that ambiguity. Or perhaps mixed messages are inevitable whenever the conversation turns to remnants. Judgment cannot be denied. Hope cannot be set aside.

Remnants presume judgment, for clearly a remnant is not the whole. Amos portrays the mathematics of the remnant in this image: "The city that marched out a thousand shall have a hundred left" (Amos 5:3). *Remnant* recalls in haunting fashion the narrative of Noah. Only a few survive. Parallel to God's insight into the human heart's inclination after the flood (Gen. 8:21), Isaiah hints that the remnant cannot claim survival on the basis of greater fidelity. The ones who survive, in Isaiah's estimation, "will no more lean on the one who struck them, but will lean on the Lord" (Isa. 10:20). Apparently the remnant leaned in the wrong direction as well—and yet, by the grace of God, the remnant survives in order to be formed by God into a new community.

That is why *remnant*, even in the harshest of prophetic texts, continues to sound a word of hope. It may be only a remnant, but a remnant will survive; a remnant will return. Even in the face of judgment, even in the presence of tragedy, the remnant serves as a promise that all is not lost. God can bring new life out of pain and unexplainable turns of events. But that will happen only if we own the reality of such suffering rather than deny it or thrust it upon others in retaliation.

To be spiritually formed by Isaiah's word of the remnant involves a willingness to trust in the Holy One through times of upheaval, whether personal or societal. We may not emerge through such crises whole, at least in terms of how and who we are at the present. We may be changed. We may find cherished parts of our lives cut loose or cut off. For some persons and for some communities, losing a part of the whole of life becomes occasion to curse the rest of life. Grief can do that. Hate can do that. Nostalgia can do that.

Isaiah's word of the remnant and our trust in the God of remnants do not come easily. Yet both come with promise: the promise that we may find renewal when loss or change leaves us less than whole; the promise that God can weave the frayed and worn remnants of our lives into new persons and new communities—and new wholeness.

> *Holy God, teach me to lean on you. May I see wholeness not merely in what is now, but in what you can make of life. And in what you can make of life, O God, make me both witness and a sign. Amen.*

SPIRITUAL EXERCISE

In your journal, reflect on a situation of grief or loss that confronted you with living a "remnant" of your previous life. In what ways did your faith find testing and/or strengthening through the experience? Read Isaiah 10:20-23. Consider your congregation and your wider community. Where do you see people confronting or denying the loss of a previous "whole" and struggling to live with "remnants" of what had been? Be at prayer for faithfulness in those situations.

DAY 3

✦

Make Us Happy

JEREMIAH 5:30-31; 6:13-14

*The prophets prophesy falsely, and the priests rule as the prophets
direct; my people love to have it so.—Jeremiah 5:31*

A S A CHILD, I can remember bumps and scrapes that brought
tears. I can also remember my mother exercising great
sympathy—if the truth be told, sympathy way out of propor-
tion to the actual wounding. A word, a kiss, and in those years
things did seem suddenly to get better. She made me happy. A
word, a kiss, and I would go back out to play, oblivious to what
had only moments before sent me racing through the door in
pain. It was enough. Then.

I write these words the day before voting booths open
across my state and country. I know this to be true for two reasons besides the calendar. First, I received phone calls yesterday
(taped messages, actually) from a United States senator and the
head of a statewide law enforcement agency. I have never
before had conversation with either of these two persons. And
second, today, television bellows polls and debates and projec-
tions and promises. Oh, Lord, the promises!

So what connects these first two paragraphs to each other
as well as to the revelations of a Jew dead now for almost
twenty-six hundred years about the state of his society?

A word, a kiss, and make the pain go away. Make us happy. Again.

Forgive me if that sounds cynical. I do not intend cynicism. I truly believe that many, maybe most, persons who serve in or seek public office do so with the best of intentions. I even believe the same about those who seek office in the church! But the problem comes in what expectations we levy upon those who would lead us. We want them to solve our problems for us, if at all possible without our involvement (certainly not our sacrifice). We want no words to pass from their mouths that would cause distress, guilt, or change to our privileges of status quo. We prefer liberals berating conservatives and conservatives haranguing liberals. That way, we can shake our heads and wonder what is wrong with those people—as in persons who do not share my enlightened views. We seek simple solutions: a word, a kiss that will make it all better. If such things are not forthcoming, then at least make us think they are.

Jeremiah might well have penned the previous paragraph. The judgment he pronounces falls on a society and religious community that operates by those same rules. In the face of grievous wounds and serious problems, Israel's leaders plaster over the crisis with the appearance of "all is well." Or to render that in more biblical terms: "They have treated the wound of my people carelessly, saying 'Peace, peace,' when there is no peace" (6:14). But the people of Israel do not resent this distortion of reality, which prevents dealing with what has gone haywire within. Instead, they "love to have it so" (5:31). My, we say, what is wrong with those people?

Those people? Ask someone today why campaign promises have become a mockery when no one seems to hold promise makers accountable. Ask someone today why we only want to hear that things will be all right for us. Ask why no one campaigns on how things are not all right for the fourteen million

Africans projected to die in the coming year because of famine. That number is approximately the equivalent of a World Trade Center attack every day—*every day*—for a year.

Perhaps these matters sound alien to concerns about spiritual formation. If so, remember Jeremiah pronounces the breach of Israel's covenant with God in the language of social dis-ease. "They do not judge with justice the cause of the orphan. . . . they do not defend the rights of the needy" (5:28). Jeremiah reveals that spirituality and conducting life as political and social persons (and communities) cannot be separated. Now as then, some offer soothing words that all is right with the world as long as all is right with me and mine. Now as then, Jeremiah insists on the truth that ignoring the vulnerable among us ignores God (see also Matt. 25:45).

A word and a kiss are not always enough to cover or heal wounds. To speak as if such wounds do not exist denies the truth of this world's suffering and sufferers. To admit such truth may not make us happy. But if such truth spurs us to faithfulness, to decrying the absence of peace rather than glibly reciting its false presumption, then the discomfort will be worth it.

> *Forgive me, O God, when I find it easier to go with the flow than to question where the flow is going and at whose expense. Amen.*

SPIRITUAL EXERCISE

Reread Jeremiah 5:30-31 and 6:13-14. What have these words to do with the life you see unfolding in your community, in your congregation, in the wider world? Reflect on at least one specific way in each of those settings you could involve yourself to some degree in truth telling. Record your reflections in your journal. Be in prayer for the strength and courage to make such witness and to find others who might share it with you.

DAY 4

✦

Wishful Believing

JEREMIAH 27:1-7; 28:1-17

. . . you made this people trust in a lie.—*Jeremiah 28:15*

NOT EVERY CLAIM of "thus says the Lord" and not everyone who appropriates such authority for his or her words merits trust. How do we know who or what to believe?

That is precisely the dilemma raised by this pair of narratives. In the first text Jeremiah constructs and wears a yoke to symbolize God's judgment soon to fall for a second time upon Judah. Jeremiah even insists the invading king and conqueror, Nebuchadnezzar, should be served, for God has deemed this Gentile enemy "my servant." In direct contradiction, the prophet Hananiah declares the yoke Jeremiah parades around to be but a temporary inconvenience. Within two years, all will be restored. God will break the yoke of Babylon. Just to make sure people see as well as hear this word, Hananiah takes Jeremiah's yoke and breaks it.

Both prophets claim the mantle "thus says the Lord." Who do we believe?

Given the distance of time and history and the twenty-twenty vision that accompanies hindsight, our answer comes easily. Hananiah's words proved wishful thinking. A two-year inconvenience became a sixty-year imposition. An entire generation, as in the wilderness sojourn, wandered outside the bounds of Promised Land and cherished Temple. Hananiah had it all wrong. Jeremiah had it all right. From our vantage point, nothing could be clearer. But no one in Jeremiah's day had that vantage point. They only had the words and the signs.

How would you decide between the two?

The question is not academic. Rival visions of the future within and without the church abound in our day. As they did in Jeremiah's time, these visions vie for our allegiance and our following. Jeremiah 27:13 spells out the disturbing implication of Jeremiah's vision: Resistance, as in rebellion or forming rival alliances against Babylon, is futile. Why? Judah's adversary is not so much Nebuchadnezzar as it is the Sovereign God who acts as God sees fit (27:5).

Hananiah rejects that theology. God will break the yoke of Babylon. The exiles will soon return. Land and people will be whole again. Some see Hananiah as opportunistic, tailoring his words to fit the ears of his audience. It need not be so. Hananiah speaks out of a theological tradition valued in Israel and in our own time. Hananiah speaks of a God irrevocably committed to a chosen people, a God who will always rescue and never disappoint. Had not God intervened when the Assyrian army threatened to overrun Jerusalem a century earlier in 701 BCE? Would God not do now what God had done before?

So cast off the advantage of hindsight and ask yourself: Who would I believe? A prophet who declares my hated enemy serves as the agent of God in turmoil or a prophet who says the suffering will not be long and God will restore those things I hold most important?

Allowing these texts to shape our spirituality necessitates taking a deep breath and recognizing that wishful believing rings as hollow as wishful thinking. Time-honored theology can mislead if it is not attuned to the unanticipated workings of God in current occasions. "God moves in a mysterious way" is not just a hymn title. Those words confess God's freedom to move outside the boundaries of religious comfort zones to create new things. They acknowledge God's freedom to do so through persons and movements we may perceive as "enemy."

To return to the initial question of this reading: How do we know who or what to believe when we hear "thus says the Lord"? God does not coerce our conclusions. They remain matters of personal trust and choice. But if we would follow Jeremiah's lead, we must not reject out of hand messages and messengers that sound out of sync with conventional wisdom, religious and otherwise. Pay close attention when self-interest or institutional survival go ignored and costs loom high for believing and acting in ways that run counter to prevailing winds. Take note when God's sovereignty holds sway far more than human cleverness or power. And pray for wisdom that, as Paul once intimated, seems foolishness in the world's eye. Such foolishness comes in the power of God to do the unexpected thing through the unexpected one.

> *Help me, O God, to be more than wishful in my believing. Help me to see your hand moving in unexpected places, to hear your voice sounding in unexpected persons—and then, to follow. Amen.*

SPIRITUAL EXERCISE

Read Jeremiah 27:1-7 and 28:1-17. Ask yourself: *With whom do I identify in these episodes? Why?* Note in your journal how you see these scenes and their dynamics reflected in present-day life. *How might God be working contrary to expectations in that setting? Why?* Pray for this situation and for your (and others') openness to God's freedom and movement.

DAY 5

Fads, Infatuations, and Faithlessness

EZEKIEL 33:30-33

To them you are like a singer of love songs . . . they hear what you say, but they will not do it.—Ezekiel 33:32

AN ASSOCIATE PROFESSOR at a midwestern university gained overnight notoriety one fall in the late 1960s. His catapult into limelight resulted, as I recall, from his indictment of an appalling lack of emphasis on classical studies in undergraduate education. One of the state's premier newspapers featured him in a prominent article. He was a hot item on campus whose presence immediately lent credibility to any gathering. People hung on his every word.

For a while. Interest waned. Fascination cooled. The professor had enjoyed what one social critic would describe as life's fifteen minutes of fame. The crowd moved to another voice. For a while.

The story repeats itself in practically every arena of life. Style of clothing, design of cars, age-targeted advertisements, diets: Fads and infatuations flow with regularity among us, including the church. Today's PowerPoint–led worship, the near-canonical status of the Left Behind novels, my generation's folk-music services and encounter groups. We cannot help but want to stay current with what is "in" to give off the aura of relevancy.

To a point the effort has merit. The church has suffered more than infrequently from an inability to relate to contemporary life. On the other hand, the church has frequently raced from one new technological gadget for liturgy or administration to another new style of liturgy or counseling. People may bounce from this preacher to that teacher as the current "guru" depending on who garners the best crowds or sells the most books. When the numbers go down, people move on.

Nothing new here. Ezekiel faced the same dilemma. Read again the lines from Ezekiel in today's text. He is the fresh, albeit disturbing, voice among the exiles in Babylon. The crowds are coming. People are turning out. Perhaps they've had to change the schedule from one to two services to accommodate the interest. Maybe even the offerings are up. Maybe. But Yahweh, speaking to the prophet for his own good, hits the nail on the head. "To them you are like a singer of love songs, one who has a beautiful voice and plays well on an instrument; they hear what you say, but they will not do it."

Why would people not follow the voice or emulate the words of one who sounds so good? For the same reason you might attend a concert by a group or artist whose lifestyle you have no interest in duplicating. It's entertainment! If you read a lot of Ezekiel, you might wonder just how folks could have mistaken him for a singer of love songs. But that's the problem when it comes to faith at times. The words may sound so good, so polished, or so well-done that people admire them—or at least the one who so crafts them—rather than embody them.

I truly believe in my heart of hearts that contemporary worship these days offers much to people who find liturgical worship a bore (and they are legion). But I also believe in my heart of hearts that the practitioners will have to wrestle against the twin seductions of worship as entertainment and leadership as celebrity cult.

Ezekiel has his hand on the pulse of a truth not altogether popular among some religious communicators. Just because someone can gather a crowd to hear the word of God doesn't mean anybody is listening. Getting someone to pay lip service takes no great effort. Being smooth, attractive, and appealing to the targeted audience will achieve that goal.

Faithfulness, on the other hand, means going deeper than passing fads. Did you notice that God addresses Ezekiel, not the faddists? Human inclinations toward infatuations are not going to change any time soon. So God prepares the prophet, and through him, prepares us. Don't be swept up by appearances that the word's getting through when actually just the style of presentation draws the attention. The word comes to life not merely in the hearing but in the doing. Those who have ears, let them hear . . . and do!

> *Holy God, constant in your mercy and grace, deliver me from inconstancy of spirit. May your word heard become your word done: in attitude, in expression, in action. In Jesus Christ. Amen.*

SPIRITUAL EXERCISE

Read Ezekiel 33:30-33. When do you find yourself expressing beliefs or opinions that you do not live out in everyday actions? In your journal, reflect on how this text addresses those aspects of your life. What disciplines of spirit or mind might be of help in moving toward change? Pray for God's leading in that renewal. If you have time, do this same exercise with your church in mind.

DAY 6

✦

The End of Abusive Power

EZEKIEL 34:1-10

I am against the shepherds; and I will . . . put a stop to
their feeding the sheep.—Ezekiel 34:10

A PARENT HAS THE power to break the spirit of a rebellious young child. A scientist has the power to clone human tissue and perhaps in the not so distant future (if not already) a human being. A community has the power to legislate the subjugation of an unwanted minority. A nation has the power to decimate an enemy's land and population. But does possession of such power justify its exercise? Just because something can be done doesn't always mean it should be done. The possession of power—be it technological or relational, legalistic or militaristic—confronts individuals and communities with hard decisions. What forms the boundary lines for power's use?

Ezekiel 34 brings a hard word to Israel's "shepherds." Biblical commentators generally agree that the primary "targets" indicted here are Judah's kings. In the final years before exile, corruption and abuse stained their exercise of power. The prophet does not mince words about these kings. Those who hoped Israel's restoration would support a revival of the monarchy found little solace in Ezekiel's truth telling.

In listening to Ezekiel's indictment of these shepherd-kings, we may say they got just what they deserved. Perhaps we cast a suspicious eye at individuals seated among the high and mighty of our day and let out a sigh of relief that Ezekiel leaves us thankfully off the hook. But does he?

The shepherds find themselves indicted, among other things, for feeding themselves instead of the sheep. The word-play in Hebrew escapes us in English: *raah*, the word for shepherd, means "to feed." Those intended to feed the flock have, instead, fed off it.

Who depends on being fed by us? Whose life counts upon our sustaining theirs to one degree or another? Who relies upon being fed, and not fed upon, by us? Parents have children or their aging parents. Employers have employees. Church leaders, ordained or not, have church persons under their charge. Teachers have students and sometimes vice versa. The list goes on. You probably can find yourself on both sides of that equation: as one who depends on the nurture of others and as one depended upon to nurture.

The word God brings through Ezekiel speaks to us as well as to Judah's shepherds. The word God brings through Ezekiel in verse 3 still decries taking the best for ourselves and leaving others to fend for themselves (see also 34:18). The word God brings through Ezekiel in verse 4 still condemns ignoring the vulnerable and lording it over those without strength or wholeness to respond. Just because we have the power to do what we choose does not mean any choice will please God. Might does not make right, whether in relations among nations or interactions among persons. Abusive power will not stand forever. God is against such shepherding.

"I am against the shepherds." Sometimes in Sunday school, it may have seemed like God was for everybody and everything. Jesus loves *all* the little children. How can God be against anybody? God does not countenance everything under the sun because of the flock, because of the vulnerable, because of needs for feeding, nurturing, justice, and mercy. God does not hold to feeding off the flock. God does not hold to acting in unloving ways toward the little children of the world, figuratively or literally. God is against those who feed off others or feast while the little ones go unfed in body or in spirit.

Yet God's word against the shepherds brings not only indictment but hope. On God's part, the hope is expressed in "I will rescue my sheep." On our part, the hope is that we can change. We can feed and we can shepherd those entrusted to our care. We can, by God's grace, if we will.

Feed my sheep. So Ezekiel urged Israel. So Jesus commissioned Peter at the end of John's Gospel. So we still hear God's call and commission to us. Feed my sheep.

Nourish me, O God, that I may see how to nurture others. Feed me with manna sufficient for the day, that I may adequately and justly feed those who depend on me. Amen.

SPIRITUAL EXERCISE

In your journal, name the persons who "feed" you in body, in spirit, in emotion. How do they do so? Next, describe those who look to you for nurture. Reread Ezekiel 34:1–10. Pray for guidance and resolve to take greater care of those persons who need you as you are able and offer thanks for the feeding you receive from others and in Christ.

✦

Introduction to Weeks 4–6

When Babylon finally destroyed Jerusalem in 587 BCE after a failed revolt, exile began in earnest. An earlier population carried into captivity to Babylon in 597 BCE found itself joined by thousands of other captives from Jerusalem and Judea. Exile, however, presented an even more fragmenting crisis than this shorthand description. Not all residents of Judah had been killed or transported to Babylon. A large group had fled to Egypt, taking Jeremiah against his will with them. Pockets of Jews survived and remained in the conquered home territory.

More than a century earlier (722 BCE), the conquest and resettlement of the Northern Kingdom had created the "ten lost tribes of Israel." Those carried away or dispersed at that time never regrouped. Legends persist to this day about remnant populations of Jewish tribes in India, Africa, and Japan, some of them the subject of modern-day DNA and linguistic sleuthing. But Israel, as a community, had disappeared. The dispersion following 587 BCE threatened Judah with the same fate.

So when Ezekiel and Jeremiah and Isaiah spoke words of hope, they doubtless encountered the deafening roar of "things as they are." Perhaps you have heard that sound as well. "You've got to be kidding!" "Be realistic." "This is how it is and how it's going to stay." "Accept it." "Get used to it." "Deal with it." Hope may generate crisis if it seems too incredible to believe, much less act on.

Hope may also generate crisis if it attempts to break a cycle that has become numbing but at least familiar in its routine.

Despair resists hope—out of past disappointments, out of a weariness that precludes thinking or doing anything other than what is known. Resignation resists hope—out of perceiving as normative what the present alone seems to dictate, out of fear to trust a future at odds with the present. When someone infuses hope into persons who are despairing of yet resigned to the way things are, a crisis results. The crisis begins when people consider risking the known for the promised.

The remaining weeks will explore words of hope from Ezekiel, Jeremiah, and Isaiah. Those words still invite persons and communities to live on the basis of God's promises. The themes organizing these weeks speak to three critical movements: "Speaking Hope to Vulnerability," "Making Room for Possibilities," and "Turning Toward Promise." The biblical texts once addressed the realities of a particular group of Jewish exiles living in a distant time and place. But in terms of life situation and issues of spiritual formation, the words speak uncannily "on target" when it comes to our own struggles to accept and embody genuine hope.

For example, sixth-century BCE Jewish exiles are not the only people who wonder if the world can ever change beyond its present ways. A not-uncommon conversation in our day about the Israeli-Arab conflict will have words and logic that run something like this: *What's the hope for peace there? Those people have been killing each other since the beginning of time. It'll never change.*

Genuine hope relies on healthy memories. To return to the Israeli-Arab conversation: "Those" people have not been killing each other since the beginning of time. If the old stories are true, those people belonged to the same family, at least until the time of Abraham's two sons Isaac and Ishmael. For centuries, Jews suffered under persecutions and inquisitions levied upon them in "Christian" Europe. During that same time, Muslim North Africa and the Ottoman Empire offered safe havens for Judaism to survive and flourish in the heart of Islamic states and culture. History is not necessarily destiny, but history can offer a hopeful perspective for those who forget that their life span does not encompass all human experience.

The prophets of the Exile not only understand that value of history; they preach it. They employ sacred history as the means to stir hope. *Do you remember Egypt and Exodus?* they plead. *And if so, can you not believe a new deliverance? Do you remember God's hand in creation? And if so, can you not imagine re-creation? Have you not known? Have you not heard?* These prophets have long memories, old stories, and living history at their command. They use them to speak seditious words intended to break the stranglehold of the present ("there is nothing new under the sun") upon the future ("God is about to do a new thing"). Such words still address persons and communities who live only for the present.

The prophets know that hope is more than the sum of what today can offer. The prophets know that hope's only limits reside in the imagination and purpose of God. God will do what God will do, whether or not it fits into the intent of Babylonian captors, the day's conventional wisdoms, or the barriers people routinely impose upon themselves. Hope says there is more. And in the saying, hope invites persons not only to trust but to act upon that promissory truth. Such hope can stir crisis when it encounters forces wishing to remain undisturbed.

The prophets themselves intentionally link hope with crisis. Earlier we saw that the prophets at times create crisis. Why should an Ezekiel or a Jeremiah or an Isaiah think it necessary to force a crisis of hope upon a community? More often than we might like to admit, life can be easier if we do not have hope. Without hope, we can just shrug our shoulders and walk away when life falls apart or when it appears the world truly is going to hell in a handbasket. For hopelessness says, *What did you expect?* Without hope, we have no motivation to think or act as if it could be otherwise.

With hope, we expect better. With hope, justice and compassion are not pipe dreams but integral parts of the life God intends for all. Because of hope, we cannot just walk away when justice and compassion go denied by persons and institutions that would prefer to keep things in their favor. Perhaps in our lifetime the hope will not come to complete fruition. Certainly the visions of restoration announced by these prophets more than two and a half millennia ago still await complete fulfillment. But hope insists we cannot wait until the whole is restored before making an effort. Or as a character in a recent movie argued, "You can't change the world, but you can make a dent." Hope invigorates persons and communities of faith to make dents, small and large, in things as they are, shaping them toward things as God intends them to be.

Words of hope make it possible for persons and communities to hear anew in whose image we are made, by whose grace we are loved, and toward whose realm creation moves. Once we truly hear (in Hebrew, the same word means both "hear" and "obey"), we are able to live in a different way. That is the crisis of hope these weeks explore.

WEEK FOUR

Speaking Hope to Vulnerability

DAY I

✦

The Promise of
Restorative Power

EZEKIEL 34:11-16

I myself will be the shepherd of my sheep.—Ezekiel 34:15

THE SANCTUARY IN a church I once served had doors with
hinges that allowed them to swing freely both ways. You
might see such doors connecting the kitchen with the dining
area in a restaurant. Waiters bring out food and buspersons
return dirty dishes by walking through without having to stop
and pull the door toward them.

Think of Ezekiel 34 as a passage so hinged. Its opening ten
verses declare God's judgment against those who exercise abusive power, feeding off the ones they were intended to nourish. This book you read now swings the opposite direction,
toward passages related to hope. The pivot occurs in this same
chapter of Ezekiel. Once again, the prophet addresses power.
But now he speaks of the power promised in God's restoration
and nourishment of a scattered people. Judgment and hope,
abusive power and restorative power, all flow closely bunched
together in Ezekiel 34. Compare verse 4 with verse 16. All but
one of the reasons given for judgment on Israel's shepherds are
now mirrored, in reverse order, in the promises of what God
will do:

"You have not strengthened the weak."—"I will strengthen the weak."

"You have not bound up the injured."—"I will bind up the injured."

"You have not brought back the strayed."—"I will bring back the strayed."

"You have not sought the lost."—"I will seek the lost."

This is not just poetic parallelism; it is poetic justice. "I will feed them with justice," Ezekiel hears God saying. Hope takes root in the promise of justice.

For whom would these words come as promise both then and now? This week focuses on hope brought to persons in vulnerable positions. Listen again to those for whom God's shepherding brings restoration: the scattered, the lost, the strayed, the injured, the weak. For persons and communities who find themselves abandoned, at risk, susceptible to being preyed upon, Ezekiel 34 invokes the image of God as shepherd. As Ezekiel has already made clear, this reference is not just "pastoral" in tone. God as shepherd promises a reshuffling of powers—political and social powers. To those without hope, God brings the promise of restoration through God's own shepherding.

One cannot neglect the societal implications, given Ezekiel's use of the shepherd/king metaphor. To keep faith with the God who makes such promises leads to keeping faith with the actions and hope promised in Ezekiel's words. In *The New Interpreter's Bible*, Katheryn Pfisterer Darr notes, "How a society and its leaders treat those who struggle against disadvantages speaks volumes about that society's true values."

On a more personal note, Ezekiel 34 invokes a humility on our spiritual journey. We do not always encounter God from positions of strength and control. Illness, fatigue, conflict, aging: all take their toll. For persons who define their identity by productivity, who always help but never receive help, experiencing vulnerability may provoke a crisis of hope, if not faith itself. If that has ever been true for you, listen to Ezekiel 34:11-16. You have not failed God because you have proved yourself human. You simply have arrived at the point of needing a shepherd through times and places of susceptibility.

In the final verse of our text, there is a significant disagreement among the Hebrew manuscripts. In the main manuscript tradition, the verse reads: "the fat and strong I will destroy [*asmid*]." Other manuscripts read: "the fat and the strong I will watch over [*asmir*]." "Destroy" returns us to the swinging door image of Ezekiel 34, where judgment and hope seem perilously close to each other. Certainly the punishment of the shepherds in the opening ten verses argues for this interpretation. But what if "watch over" reveals another truth about God's restorative power? Namely, God does care for and restore the vulnerable, but even those of power and strength have a place within God's care. For the vulnerable, God's shepherding extends in nurturing. For the powerful, God's shepherding watches over to prevent abuse of that strength.

However we interpret that word and its meaning for journey with God, the final phrase wraps all together in a clear affirmation. "I will feed them with justice." Whether we count ourselves among the vulnerable or the powerful, among the weak or the strong, God's justice will prevail in gathering the scattered and restoring life. So begins our journey toward hope.

> *Shepherd me, O God. Feed me where I truly hunger. Bind me up where I am torn. Strengthen me where my weakness prevails. And watch over me with your care. Amen.*

SPIRITUAL EXERCISE

Read Ezekiel 34:16. In your journal, write down those whose faces or situations come to mind as you read those words. Pray for them. Note ways you might be of service to them. Now reread the verse with yourself in mind. How does this verse reflect your own experience of God? Offer thanks for God's shepherding.

DAY 2

✦

Trust and Peace

EZEKIEL 34:25-31

*They shall live in safety, and no one shall make
them afraid.—Ezekiel 34:28*

SAFETY. SECURITY. LET those two words drift through your
mind and heart for a moment. What images do they evoke?
For some, it might be the embrace of a loved one or the sanctuary of a favored place. For others, it could be the vigilance
of law enforcement or the capability of military personnel. But
for all, safety and security engender a sense of well-being
where fear relinquishes its hold—or perhaps where we find
ourselves able to loose our hold on fear. How do you let go of
fear? One answer comes in being able to trust. In order to feel
safe, in order to experience security, you must be able to trust
in something or someone greater than yourself, greater than
your fears.

In order to feel safe and secure in the world, children need
to trust caretakers who provide for their needs, including the
need to be loved. In order to feel safe and secure in relationships, adults need to trust their partners to do right by them,
including living without fear in that relationship. In order to
feel safe and secure in life, all persons need to know they can

extend trust and not be betrayed or rejected. Safety, security, and trust weave together. The quest in life is to answer the question: Who finally can be deemed trust*worthy*?

"I will make with them a covenant of peace," Ezekiel begins in our reading. The prophet goes on to identify what sorts of things will make for *shalom*. This Hebrew word signifies not just an absence of war but a wholeness of life voided of need and fear. Continuing previous affirmations in this chapter, Ezekiel couches covenant's promise in shepherding imagery: land, water, pasture, an absence of devouring animals. But also tucked in these verses are the words that opened this meditation. For this flock will "sleep in the woods *securely*"; "be *secure* on their soil"; "live in *safety*" (verses 25, 27, 28; italics added). Those with whom God enters covenant and offers the gift of shalom will be safe and secure.

So how will they—or we—know and accept that dual promise of safety and security? Those two words in English translate a single Hebrew word, *betach*, whose underlying meaning is "confidence" or "trust." In other words, we could justifiably say that a state of safety or security requires a state of trust. Outward trappings do not guarantee the safety or security of an individual or community. Many folks in this world live serene lives in absolutely terrifying situations because they exercise trust. Other folks flounder within anxiety-ridden lives while surrounded by great wealth, powerful armies, and the best home security systems money can buy.

You cannot buy trust.

If Ezekiel is right, then you also cannot buy safety and security. For in the end, trust and safety and security are one and the same. To be sure, you can put your trust in wealth and might. You can stake your confidence in all the technological doodads and measures of material wealth your heart desires. But the prophets, Ezekiel among them, constantly turn Israel back to the question of, and the quest for, who finally can be deemed trustworthy. And for the prophets, Ezekiel among them, all other objects of trust pale in light of God, whose safety and security will not disappoint those who trust in God. "They shall know that I, the LORD their God, am with them, and that they, the house of Israel, are my people."

Do you trust that word?

God promises the gift of shalom to those who hear that word and say: There will be my safety. There will be my security. There will be my trust.

So help me, God.

> *Keep me from seeking safety and security in places that will disappoint. Help me, rather, to trust in you. For you will be enough. For now. For all time. For all creation. Amen.*

SPIRITUAL EXERCISE

Reread Ezekiel 34:30. Reread it aloud a second time, substituting "you" for "they/them," "your" for "their," your name for "the house of Israel," and "child" for "people." In your journal, write what that affirmation suggests to you about your life and your trust. Read it again. Offer thanks for the gift of God's presence.

DAY 3

Grace in the Wilderness

JEREMIAH 31:1-14

*The people who survived the sword found grace
in the wilderness.—Jeremiah 31:2*

WILDERNESS TODAY IS marketable. I do not mean that only in the sense of ever-raging political battles over opening pristine areas to commercial development. I'm also referring to the attraction wilderness holds for people in suburbanized societies like ours. We see wilderness as a welcome companion. This appeal is summoned up in peculiar ways sometimes. A television commercial pictures a tranquil forest, complete with trout stream and deer. Then an SUV rolls into view, disgorging khaki-clad seekers of wildness. There's no small irony in a love of wilderness so easily entered—and so quickly left if wild becomes more than a prefix.

Wilderness had no such appeal to Jeremiah's audience. Earlier, wilderness had been the maze for forty years of wandering. Now hundreds of miles of desert steppes separated exiles from homeland. Wilderness was not the desired destination of smiling-faced and well-fed backpackers out to renew the human spirit. Wilderness loomed as the potential killing grounds of those too slow to escape the captors and those too weak to finish the journey even if escape could be made.

So it comes as something of a surprise that Jeremiah 31 begins a message of hope with words that might have seemed self-contradicting: "grace in the wilderness." Wilderness represented less a font of grace and more a levy of punishment. Earlier portions of Jeremiah and other prophets describe Israel's wilderness predicament of exile as a result of God's judgment rather than favor. But God does not rest content to persist in judgment. Into wilderness, into exile, will come a word of grace. God will be present. God will act in love.

God. To a people lost in wilderness, lost in exile, lost in the recognition of punishment, God might be one of the first pieces of baggage jettisoned to lighten the load. Exile, and its wilderness, is not limited to a portion of the Jewish people in the sixth century before Christ. Exile, and its wilderness, occurs whenever we find ourselves separated from our usual points and persons of reference. In that separation, we can easily wonder what has become of God. Wilderness seems to deny God, at least a God of compassion or caring—or grace. How can we speak of God when such things happen? How can we hope in God when all around is hopelessness?

When Jeremiah asserts "grace in the wilderness," we wonder how that can be. When God seems absent from what has befallen us, where is the grace in that? When has grace ever been found in the wilderness? Exodus 33. The golden calf had been fashioned and worshiped. The people were sent packing from Sinai with the chilling word that God would not be making the trip with them (33:3). Moses intercedes. How does God respond? "My presence will go with you, . . . for you have found favor [the same word in Jeremiah is translated 'grace'] in my sight" (vv. 14, 17).

The grace in the wilderness of Exodus 33 is the presence of God who will make the journey with the people. The grace in the wilderness in Jeremiah 31 is the presence of God who will make possible this new journey out of exile with the people. Grace in the wilderness today remains the promised gift of God's presence on the journeys we make.

Make no mistake: Every one of those journeys remains fraught with difficulties. Exodus 33 came at the beginning, not the end, of forty years of wandering. Jeremiah 31 still faced the long road home—and once there, the even longer task of rebuilding. And today? We do not yet live in the realized sovereign realm of God on earth. Our journeys as individuals, as communities, still pass through hard and dangerous places, places that may very well look and act like wilderness.

But here is the gift, here is the promise, here is the grace for our wilderness: God will journey with us. God will make that journey not as punitive taskmaster but as gracious sustainer. God will journey with us as God always has—with steadfast love, with everlasting love. The past is prelude. The future is promised. Grace can be found in the wilderness.

> *God, may your presence sustain me. By cool waters and pleasant pastures, by rushing torrents and barren rockscapes. In community and in wilderness, guide my faith with your love. Amen.*

SPIRITUAL EXERCISE

Recall places and times of wilderness in your life: places that threatened separation from community and God, places that tested your trust and hope. Reread Jeremiah 31:2. In your journal, reflect on what "grace(s)" you discovered in such wilderness and how you discovered grace. Offer a prayer of thanks for God's presence in all of your journeys. Pray for another who passes now through a wilderness time.

DAY 4

✦

The Future in Earnest

JEREMIAH 32:5-15, 42-44

*Houses and fields and vineyards shall again
be bought in this land.—Jeremiah 32:15*

IN 1999 MY WIFE and I became first-time home buyers. In
the process leading up to that, we experienced many
"dances" with which you may be familiar. Inspections and
appraisals. Offers and counteroffers. And finally, earnest money,
that payment made as a pledge to the seriousness of the buyer.
With earnest money, you don't own anything yet, but there is
the hope that this home eventually will be yours, once all the
contractual hassles find resolution.

Earnest money.

The armies of Babylon flooded the countryside of Judea
and laid siege to Jerusalem itself. Jeremiah sat in prison, under
orders of King Zedekiah of Judah, for the unpatriotic audacity
of declaring that both Jerusalem and Zedekiah would fall.
What did Jeremiah do from the captivity of prison? The
prophet plopped down earnest money (actually, the entire purchase price!) for a piece of land owned by his cousin.

The act was absurd on several counts. Jeremiah's imprison-
ment on direct order of the king did not lend itself to imminent hope for taking a stroll on the new property anytime

soon. Even if he could have, a trip to the field would have placed the prophet square in the middle of a Babylonian battalion. Invading armies tend to have little regard for property deeds. Possession is nine-tenths of the law—or more.

On the surface, the cousin of Jeremiah seems to have made the better deal. He's got cash in hand in exchange for land occupied by the enemy. The spirit of Jeremiah's cousin lives on in attitudes and actions that disregard long-term concerns for short-term gains. So what if we sacrifice the long-term stability of public education, social services, and the environment for a few extra bucks today? The future is now, so let's get what we can, cut our losses, and let others worry about (and pay) the consequences.

Jeremiah hands over good money for something that may never benefit him during his lifetime. But that is exactly the point. Indeed, that is exactly God's purpose. The only justification for Jeremiah's action lies in hope rooted in the future. Such hope forms the core of verse 15's promise: "Houses and fields and vineyards shall again be bought in this land." Because there is hope, Jeremiah puts down earnest money on the future.

So what of us? The spirit of our age dwells on what is now and immediate. The spirituality urged by Jeremiah 32 invokes a different orientation about faith and time. Our trust in God's transforming presence encompasses the future every bit as much as the present. Faith neither sells out the future for the present nor vice versa. Faith acts now for the sake of the future. Hope transforms this day by trusting it to the One who beckons us to new days.

Jeremiah's hope engages in significant risk. Jeremiah places financial resources and reputation at the disposal of a future not yet clear at best and ominous at worst. The prophet makes himself vulnerable, so that folks made vulnerable through exile will have cause to hope. What would justify that hope? In the midst of—even in contradiction of—changing and troubling circumstances, God's sovereignty and promises remain trustworthy. God holds the future in earnest by pledging to "bring upon them [us] all the good fortune that I now promise them" (Jer. 32:42).

Jeremiah ventured seventeen shekels in earnest for the hope of a God-fulfilled future. In the fullness of time, God ventured the Only Begotten as earnest for that same hope and promised future.

What would you venture for the future—in earnest?

> *God, how have you been able to risk so much for what remains in the future: in your act of Creation, in your gift of redemption, in your hopes for my life? I would know, for I would risk. Amen.*

SPIRITUAL EXERCISE

Reread Jeremiah 32:6-15, 42-44. Place yourself in Jeremiah's position. List the reasons why you should, and should not, purchase that field. Reflect in your journal how those reasons relate to your hopes and fears for the future and to the tugs and pulls of the present. Be at prayer over what you have ventured for the sake of the future in the past and for such choices that may face you now.

DAY 5

✦

Comforted and Borne

ISAIAH 40:1-11

Speak tenderly to Jerusalem.—*Isaiah 40:2*

I LOVE RELIGIOUS CHORAL music. I came up through the ranks of my home church's junior and senior choirs as a youth. My spirit has been nourished by an extraordinary choir in the community where I now live. But one of my most moving experiences of music in the last fifteen or so years occurred when I played the tape of a secular song during a church service. Our church had no choir at that time, so I augmented our music by playing publishers' demo tapes of religious songs for our "morning anthem." On that particular Sunday, for a reason I can no longer remember, I did not. Instead, I played an audiocassette tape of Simon and Garfunkel's "Bridge Over Troubled Waters." You may be familiar with it. I had heard it many times before, but I have not heard it the same since.

A woman from the congregation came up afterward and thanked me for playing that song that day. Without her saying anything further, I realized why. Recently her husband had been charged with molesting a grandchild, an act he had committed against his own children. I had sat with this woman and the children in court as her husband was sentenced. My friend had stood her ground with great courage alongside her children. She denied her husband the ability to manipulate anyone anymore, but the emotional toll had been great. That day, in her vulnerability, God spoke comfort through the words of a song.

In Isaiah God speaks comfort to people made vulnerable by exile. God "will gather the lambs in his arms, and carry them in his bosom, and gently lead the mother sheep." Tenderness and gentleness dominate the image. But do not mistake softness for weakness. God does not engage in cradling and nurturing because God is powerless to do anything else. Isaiah also reveals here: "The Lord GOD comes with might, and his arm rules for him." The God who carries lambs also shatters kingdoms. The God who tenderly leads those with young also has the capacity to drive out any and all who would oppress and hurt.

God as warrior, God as nurturer: The identities do not contradict each other. They complement and allow for each other. How could we hope for any comfort from a God unable to deal with the powers and forces that dehumanize our lives? On the other hand, why should we hope in a God who only wields power without a hint of compassion? The prophet understands Israel's need for a God strong enough to risk compassion and caring enough to risk powerful intervention on behalf of those otherwise cut off and cast adrift.

We who live in this day bear needs for ourselves and our wider society similar to Isaiah's audience. Folks still live on the margins today. Folks still go ignored and impoverished by indifferent systems of state or economy. Folks still are abused and discarded. To such as these Isaiah promises One who will gather and carry and gently lead, One with power enough to keep that promise. So who will not only bear that word but take up its actions in ministries of justice and advocacy? In other words, who will embody the grace of God? "Get you up to a high mountain," the text summons. "Comfort my people" does not merely assert God's intention. It invites our participation.

But you may say, and with justification: *The situations around us seem so hopeless. Forces arrayed against compassion and gentleness are so entrenched, so beyond our means to change.* Once again, the text invites, "Get you up to a high mountain." Isaiah 40 announces and summons changes. It declares the good news that the world has been and will be changed by God. It declares new ways for demonstrating power. No one too weak for the journey will be left behind. The One mighty enough to reduce empires to memories is the One gentle enough to gather lambs and lead those with young. God will comfort and bear us up when we do not have the strength, health, or wherewithal to do so. God will empower us to speak and trust and act the good news that fear's day is over and to live our lives accordingly.

The mouth of the Lord has so spoken. Will we?

> *In my weakness and need, O God, bear me close to your bosom. And in my strength, enable me to bear your lambs in my arms. And in all my times, may I bear witness to your grace and might. Amen.*

SPIRITUAL EXERCISE

Reread Isaiah 40:11. As you read those words, visualize a person, a group, or a people in need of God's embrace and support. In your journal, write down how you and your community might be the arms God uses to bear up those persons. Follow through. Be at prayer for God's action in the world on behalf of such persons and for faithfulness in sharing in that ministry.

DAY 6

✦

When You Pass through the Waters

ISAIAH 43:1-7

I will be with you.—Isaiah 43:2

IN THE SUMMER of 1988 my mother was diagnosed with Alzheimer's disease. That summer began for her a long, slow descent into the hell of that disease. It took her self, not just from those of us who loved her. It took her self from her. Her personality veered in directions we had never seen. Memory, then speech, then mobility dissipated. My sister kept an album of family pictures in my mother's room. Looking through the album became a standard liturgy for visits. We would look at the photographs of her as a young woman—with her brother, with my father, with me as a child. I did not know if she knew anything about the people in those images, most of all that attractive woman with the soft eyes and easy smile. Could she even recognize the presence of her self?

During those visits, in a slight smile at greeting, a quiet kiss at parting, there were times I wanted to hope that she knew me—at least that she knew I was someone once special to her. I wanted to hope that she knew I had been with her. I did not want her to be afraid anymore.

That was the child in me, hoping against hope that my just being there would help. After all, being there had often been the way in which Mom had eased my fears when I was a child. Most of my fears back then were pretty much imagined, born of nightmares or overactive imagination about what might lurk behind a closet door. On the other hand, I distinctly remember a real hospital test in a large room with strange machines. What stands in my memory, though, is not fear of that place but my mother's presence with me there. Her presence with me sufficed.

"Do not fear, for I am with you." Perhaps it was the child in Isaiah that understood the importance of pairing fear's dismissal with the assurance of presence. The text admits that God's companionship does not guarantee the end of fearful experiences. Isaiah's imagery of waters that threaten to overwhelm and fires that can burn remind us that we continue to live on the far side of God's sovereign realm. Faith's journey may yet take us through some harrowing landscapes. There are no assurances we will not encounter what might otherwise scare the best and strongest of us, and for good reason. Alzheimer's. AIDS. War. Hunger. Injustice. Just like those exiles Isaiah originally addressed, we too have cause to feel overwhelmed and seared by the pains we experience or those we suffer in compassion for others.

Yet God does not leave us alone or unaided. "I will be with you" forms but one-half the reason why our fears may subside. "Do not fear, for I have redeemed you." The language of redemption comes out of Jubilee traditions (Lev. 25:25-26, 48-49), whereby one family member intercedes on behalf of another in a more vulnerable position. The God who promises to be present with us is also the God who promises to act for us.

What actions does Isaiah 43 see God taking on our behalf? In the first instance, God calls us by name and declares us God's own (v. 1). In being named, we belong to God. In the second instance, God will gather those so named from every direction they (we) have been dispersed. In our gathering, we belong to God. Consider that gift of naming and promise for gathering in the context of fear. Fear's power relies on the threat of stripping name and place from us. In illness, in estrangement, in death: We fear the loss of who we are and those we love.

At the end of her life, my mother knew no one's name, not even her own. Yet I believe the One who once named her calls her by name now, in that place where her scattered mind and spirit have been gathered whole and new. Why do I hope in such things? With Isaiah, I believe hope comes by God's naming and gathering.

We are named by the Holy One of Israel. At the font of baptism, God names us children of grace, sons and daughters of love. And we are gathered by Christ's grace. At the Communion Table, God gathers us from every direction in which our lives have been scattered. Sometimes the scattering has been in service, sometimes in fear. Yet at that table, God invites us to come from every place to this place, where we may feast on the promise of Jesus' presence with us in this time and in all our times. For according to Isaiah, hope comes by God's naming and gathering.

What do you believe?

> *I do have fears, God. You know that, for you know me wholly. So remind me of the name you give me, remind me of the hope of gathering. For I would not fear, knowing you are with me. Amen.*

SPIRITUAL EXERCISE

Reread Isaiah 43:1-7. Think of waters you have passed through. How did (do) you experience God's presence in that ordeal? What difference has "God with you" made in other such times? Read again verse 1: "Do not fear, ... I have called you by name." Speak it aloud, and hear it as God's voice addressing you. Now. Personally. Live the rest of this day in the knowledge and hope that God has called you by name and you are God's beloved.

WEEK FIVE

Making Room for Possibilities

DAY 1

Individual Responsibility

EZEKIEL 18:1-9, 19-22

A child shall not suffer for the iniquity of a parent, nor a parent suffer for the iniquity of a child.—Ezekiel 18:20

I HAVE VAGUE RECOLLECTIONS of words spoken by elementary teachers at Baden Grade School. They went something like this: "John Indermark. So you're Jean and Janet's little brother!" In fairness to those teachers, I don't remember any particular experience of being judged by or forced to live up to the reputations of my sisters who preceded me. But such things do happen.

Some individuals are held up to a standard set by a sibling, for good or for ill. Or a child may develop a reputation early on that becomes an identity from which he or she never escapes, no matter what. I was less sensitive to this phenomenon as a child than as a parent. For some of my son's classmates, each new school year brought no new slate to relationships with teachers or administrators.

Being judged for who you used to be is no less detrimental than being judged for who you never were. Strive as you might, you do tend to give up trying to change when enough people reinforce the belief that you won't.

"'The parents have eaten sour grapes, and the children's teeth are set on edge'" (Ezek. 18:2). In the day of Ezekiel, this proverb apparently became a popular adage to explain God's handling of human sin. Long-standing traditions upheld this view: You better not mess with God because you'll ruin not only your life but the lives of your children and grandchildren. No less than the second commandment of the Decalogue given to Moses weighs in with a heavy hand: "I the LORD your God am a jealous God, punishing children for the iniquity of parents, to the third and the fourth generation of those who reject me" (Exod. 20:5). Who wants to argue with commandments once graven on stone?

Apparently God does. Read Ezekiel 18. You gain a remarkably different portrait of retributive justice than that lamented in the proverb. Responsibility is not determined by genealogy but by one's own choices in life. "A child shall not suffer for the iniquity of a parent, nor a parent suffer for the iniquity of a child; the righteousness of the righteous shall be his own" (18:20).

This text provides part of the bridge in Ezekiel from judgment to hope. Some may hear in this word an even sharper declaration of judgment. It says we are responsible for our actions. We cannot pass the blame to others, no matter how convenient or appealing a target they may provide. Where's the hope in this?

The hope stems from this passage's implication: You are free. You are free from how others keep their responsibilities or don't. You are free to get out from underneath the blame laid on you based on someone else's reputation. You are free to live as a child named by God, not one who must live up to names or stereotypes others would place as limits upon you. You are free to be responsible to God.

That freedom brings an important gift and task to spiritual formation. For in that *freedom* to develop your relationship with God, you are also *responsible* for that development. Your spiritual formation does not in the final word hinge upon the congregation in which you are involved. It does not rise or fall on the direction you receive from mentors or the group with whom you may be exploring this book. Your freedom to mature spiritually is also your responsibility to own.

That statement too may sound a note of judgment. Perhaps responsibility must always do that to a degree. But I hope you also hear in it the word of grace Ezekiel intends. For God judges neither your life nor your spirituality in comparison to someone you have never been and God never intended you to be. God simply invites you to know and serve God as you are and as God may yet transform you in newness of life. "The righteousness of the righteous shall be his [her] own." Your own . . . God's own.

> *Free me, O God, for serving you as you lead me. Save me from self-defeating comparisons of my own making or those of others. Lead me into mature responsibility for what I do and who I am. In Jesus Christ. Amen.*

SPIRITUAL EXERCISE

What comparison to others or "guilt by association" holds you back or stifles your sense of responsibility? Write down these roadblocks in your journal. Identify and reflect on specific actions you can take that might help you get past them. In prayer, seek the Holy Spirit's moving and working in you to bring a greater gift of freedom as you would take responsibility to grow in new and deeper ways in Christ.

DAY 2

✦

Rattling Dry Bones

EZEKIEL 37:1-14

*Suddenly there was a noise, a rattling, and the bones
came together.—Ezekiel 37:7*

PERHAPS YOU HAVE heard or said these words: *We've never
done it that way before.* In the distant past, some anonymous
wit tagged them as "The Seven Last Words of the Church."
Why does that statement merit such judgment? Those words
close doors to new light. Those words assume that the past will
always and everywhere dictate the future. Those words are
scriptural. "What has been is what will be, and what has been
done is what will be done; there is nothing new under the
sun" (Eccles. 1:9).

But then there are other scriptures.

The hand of God brings out Ezekiel, by spirit, to a valley
full of bones. There were very many bones. They were very
dry. If you want an image of closed doors, if you want an image
of the past always and everywhere dictating the future, look at
the bones. From dust we come; to dust we return. Whatever
hopes we claim had best find fulfillment within the bookends
of those two states of dust. For this is how we all end up: dry
bones. This is how it has always been before.

"Mortal, can these bones live?" (Ezek. 37:3)

Ezekiel's original hearers certainly knew a dead bone when they saw one. They had known the deadening of captivity. They had seen hopes dry up in exile. Some remembered sand stinging faces in a forced march from a land their children had never seen. Can these bones live?

Today we know a dead bone when we see one. Every Christmas we declare in song that "peace on the earth, goodwill to all" came upon a midnight clear. Then we resign ourselves to another year of conflicts, personal and international. We watch friends and loved ones lowered in caskets into cement-lined graves from which they do not return. We feel the tug of long-held dreams and personal aspirations running out of time, energy, or will, imposed by the horizon line in our lives. We linger in churches whose membership ages, whose youth wander elsewhere if anywhere, and whose programs and vitality suffer as a result. Can these bones live?

If the past dictates the future, if there is nothing new under the sun, quite clearly the answer is no. So we leave old, dry bones in place, not wanting to disturb their peace. God, however, is not such a contented caretaker of all that has been and thus ever shall be. If Ezekiel can be trusted, God is a troubler and disturber of bones—a grave robber really. Where bones parch dry, God breathes. Where stiffness nullifies movement, wind blows. Where hopes spill out emptied, Spirit comes and fills. Breath and wind and spirit converge for life in Ezekiel 37 as they gathered for life in Genesis 1—as they conspire for life among us today.

Ezekiel 37 illustrates a spirituality perilously open to surprise and life in the most unexpected and dead-end places and persons. In Ezekiel's day, the rattling of dry bones wakens people from the reality of exile to the possibility of return against all odds. How could Israel possibly slip free from the Babylonian Empire? How could a homeland lost become restored? What had been given up for dead with good reason now becomes possibility. In our day, the claim is no less extravagant. Ezekiel 37 witnesses to faith that steadfastly refuses to take the past or present as guarantee for what must be. Breath and wind and Spirit still have life among us, still *give* life among us. Breath and wind and Spirit, as Jesus teaches elsewhere, blow and go where God wills, not where the church presumes or controls.

What Ezekiel sees, what Ezekiel prophesies, had never been done before. It was, in contradiction to Ecclesiastes, a truly new thing under the sun. What Ezekiel sees, what Ezekiel prophesies, sets the stage for all manner of truly unbelievable turnings. Just look at the Gospels. Samaritans go commended. Gentiles go included. Sinners go graced. And Jesus' dead bones, entombed for three days, go resurrected.

Those of us who live by the watchword of never having done it that way before need to take a stroll with Ezekiel among dry bones. We need to feel earth tremble when dead-and-gone hopes acquire sinew, flesh, and spirit. In that valley God's possibilities trump every limitation history can conjure. And if dry bones can live, what about those dry and deadened places among us? "I will put my spirit within you, and you shall live."

O dry bones, hear the word of the Lord!

> *You know, O God, where hopes have gone dry in me. Breathe new life; breathe new hope that I may live by your Spirit. Amen.*

SPIRITUAL EXERCISE

Read Ezekiel 37:1-2. What in your life would comprise a view of hopes given up or aspirations denied? Read verse 9 again. How might God's moving and renewing Spirit enliven one of those hopes that you have long set aside or one that is a current struggle? Pray to discern God's renewing Spirit in that area of your life.

DAY 3

✦

Forgiveness

JEREMIAH 31:31-34

*For they shall know me, from the least of them
to the greatest.—Jeremiah 31:34*

HOW DO WE know God? My own answer evolves through
a long, ongoing story starting in early childhood and
gradually winding its way through succeeding years. Others
may identify with coming to know God in dramatically sin-
gular moments. People have shared with me experiences of
religious conversion complete with day and time of "before
and after," and I believe them. Even those of us who have perceived God more in nurture over time do have watershed
moments when our eyes have been opened and our lives
turned around.

For me, a retreat I attended in college had such an effect.
A major focus of the weekend involved "translating" Christian
theology and story into language suited to modern philosophi-
cal and sociological discourse. It was terribly interesting. But
somewhere in the middle of the retreat, the thought struck me:
*Why cast off the language? Why recast the stories? Why does the
knowledge of God have to be camouflaged for folks to accept it?*

At the heart of that realization stands our opening question: How do we know God? Leaders at that retreat made a

strategic decision in using the premise that we know God through language. The people who buttonhole us to ask, "Brother (or Sister), do you know Jesus?" may seem to emphasize experience. But they too rely on language for putting us on the spot and then arguing if we don't use their formulas for measuring faith or apostasy.

Jeremiah takes on that same question of "how do we know God" in today's text. The prophet makes enormous claims about God that stretch and eventually exceed the ability of language alone to understand how we know God. The prophet goes on to say this covenant will be written on hearts rather than engraved on stones. In other words, covenant relationship goes to the core of who we are rather than remaining a list of rules that may or may not find their way into the human heart. Such a covenant based upon externals presumed the need of "teachers" to instruct what is and is not lawful. According to Jeremiah, intrusive "know the Lord" types will no longer be needed because all will know God.

How will all come to that knowledge of God? "I will forgive their iniquity, and remember their sin no more." The knowledge of God will not come through the elegant persuasions of a pulpiteer. The knowledge of God will not come through an in-your-face style of evangelism that leaves no stone unturned and no doorstep unbothered. The knowledge of God will not even come through making sure we are kind to neighbors and responsible citizens in a Christian nation. All will come to the knowledge of God through God's forgiveness of all.

To understand the force of Jeremiah's statement, remember this is the same prophetic book that earlier declared God's intent against Israel to "remember their iniquity and punish their sins" (14:10). Exile resulted. And now, according to the same prophet, the way people—all people—will know God is through forgiveness. Forgiveness offers God's change of heart in this new covenant toward Israel. Indeed, it could be argued forgiveness is that new covenant.

You may see, then, why we look at this text in a week devoted to the theme of "making room for possibilities." Forgiveness presents the ultimate of possibilities: moving into a new future. Those who covet the status quo find forgiveness an unacceptable threat. Look at Jesus. In several instances, opponents took greater offense at his forgiving than at his healing people. Why? Forgiveness sets people free. Forgiveness makes new ways and new life possible. Forgiveness can even enact new covenants when our hearts know God through the experience of forgiveness.

But beware of spirituality rooted in forgiveness. It will not leave us unchanged. It will not let us presume that all is fixed and static. Forgiveness lets loose possibilities and futures we could not have imagined had God simply dealt with us in a just but unmerciful way. Forgiveness reopens doors—and lives—closed by unredemptive guilt.

How do we know God? Know ourselves and those we encounter as forgiven. And in such knowledge, act—and forgive—accordingly.

> *Engrave on my heart your forgiveness, O God, that I not forget its word in the embarrassment of my sin, that I do not forget its word in my venturing to forgive others. Amen.*

SPIRITUAL EXERCISE

Reread Jeremiah 31:34. Reflect on various ways and persons by whom you have come to the knowledge of God. Remember significant moments of forgiveness—received and given. In your journal, write how those moments have instructed you in the knowledge of God. Pray to be more forgiving and to be more receptive to forgiveness.

DAY 4

✦

Tenacity

JEREMIAH 36:20-32

Take another scroll and write on it all the former words that were in the first scroll.—Jeremiah 36:28

THE GREAT CATHEDRALS in Europe took decades, even centuries, to build. Generations of workers persisted in translating an architect's vision into foundation and structure. Framing, carving, glassing, painting, weaving, and other crafts converged in stunning creations such as Cologne and Chartres. Such projects cannot be undertaken by people who must see the finished product. Patience is required but not the patience of passively waiting for work to get done. Tenacity describes the ability to keep on working when the work seems never done or constantly shifting. Tenacity will not let go or give up.

Tenacity predominates in Jeremiah 36. The tenacity of Jeremiah and Baruch figures prominently. Baruch copies word for word, letter for letter, what Jeremiah dictates to him. Scribal work has been forgotten in our era of copiers and scanning machines. Look at the book you are now reading. Imagine being asked to write its contents by hand—legibly enough to read, reproducing every word and sentence exactly. Then imagine listening to someone dictate this book aloud. Your job will be to write accurately and swiftly everything that is said. The act of writing itself becomes a demonstration of tenacity, attending to every word over days and weeks until the task is over.

Imagine the tenacity required when that one handcrafted copy you have labored over is cut into strips by one who takes offense at both message and messengers. You have no choice but to start again, this time with even more words to write. Baruch and Jeremiah remain tenacious in the face of the king's response. They do not throw their hands in the air and say, in effect, you can't fight city hall. Baruch takes pen in hand; Jeremiah begins to speak; and the labor resumes. They will not give up. They remain tenacious.

Tenacity brings a unique word to a spirituality that makes room for possibilities. Possibilities do not always explode upon the scene and rush to fulfillment. Some possibilities take a good deal of tending, preparing, and laboring over before they even begin to emerge. Lyndon Johnson signed the Voting Rights Act into law in 1965. What made that day possible included school children in Little Rock, Arkansas; Rosa Parks on a bus in Alabama; protesters at lunch counters; and civil rights workers murdered in Mississippi. All those folks and more endured the resistance of powers not interested in making room for possibilities in race relations in this nation. Tenacity drove that movement to keep the dream alive in the face of water cannons, police dogs, Jim Crow policies, and church bombings. Tenacity in such circumstances equals more than patience. Tenacity involves trust in the ultimate outcome.

The trustworthiness of that outcome comes into play in another tenacity present in this passage. The prophet and the scribe are not the only two who exercise determination. The other tenacity at work here belongs to God. The struggle pits more than Jeremiah against the king. More significantly, the contest weighs the power between the king and God. The king does not like the words on the scroll, so he exercises his authority and personally sees to their destruction. But God remains tenacious. Another scroll will be produced. Not only that, it will have more to say than the first. God will not let God's purposes be set aside. For the king, that's bad news. For those who rely on God, however, God's tenacity comes as good news. Why?

God seeks us with grace tenaciously. Psalm 139, particularly verses 7–12, offers a remarkable affirmation of God's tenacity in seeking us out not for punishment but for relationship. God loves us tenaciously. How else can we describe the ministry and passion of Jesus, who forgives enemies and does not cease to love disciples who desert and deny? The tenacity of God is this: We are loved with a love that will not let us go.

So loved, may we be tenacious in our loving, in our hoping, and in our trusting God to see us through.

> *Instill in me, O God, the spirit of tenacity. I do not need stubbornness that refuses to budge. I need tenacity that moves by your Spirit's leading wherever and however you would have me go. Amen.*

SPIRITUAL EXERCISE

Reflect on one aspect of your life that has required (and may still require) tenacity on your part. Record your reflections in your journal. What in that experience involves who you are as a person of faith in terms of your hopes? in terms of your convictions? Pray for God's guidance and help in remaining tenacious. Seek discernment in how that experience may be enriched or deepened by the tenacity you see and receive from the hands and grace of God.

DAY 5

Guess Who's Coming to Worship?

ISAIAH 56:1-8

*I will gather others to them besides those
already gathered.—Isaiah 56:8*

I REMEMBER A FUROR in our congregation when I was a teenager. A civil rights activist in Saint Louis had interrupted the service at nearby Saint Matthew's Lutheran Church with a call for reparations to descendants of slaves. Much discussion followed in our congregation about what to do if "he" showed up: call the police, listen quietly, escort him out, who knows what else. He never showed, so we never had to cross that bridge.

Granted, we rarely worry these days about who may be joining us in the sanctuary come Sunday. Unless, for example, there has been an especially messy divorce between two church members, and folks choose sides. Will we sit in the same pew with him after what he did? Will we continue worshiping at the early service if she is there? Or unless, as in some quarters of the church, division arises over who (or more to the point, what kind of person) we will let into our pulpits. For some, a person of color in that position raised eyebrows and lowered contributions. For others, even the consideration of a woman as a preacher evoked not-in-my-lifetime oaths. These days persons of different sexual orientation in pulpits—and even pews—trigger the declaration of last straws and final notices for not a few.

With whom we worship does matter. We're not talking about McDonald's or White Castle, where we sit in close quarters with people we may not know and perhaps will never see again. Worship brings us into sacred place where stories form us and sacraments nourish us into one people by God's grace. The company we keep does matter.

Isaiah 56:1-8 understands that importance of place. The passage speaks to the transforming significance of hospitality in opening sacred place. At issue here is the status of foreigners and eunuchs. Banning eunuchs from religious assembly was not an isolated tradition of certain synagogues or rabbis. Deuteronomy 23:1 brings the force of Torah to bear: No eunuchs need bother knocking at the door. It is locked. And foreigners? Foreigners need not apply; they will not be welcome. Many biblical scholars believe the context for Isaiah 56 to be the time after Israel's return from exile when Israel was rebuilding physical walls and also erecting walls of exclusion, separating Jews from outsiders. This era also probably generated the books of Ruth and Jonah, both powerful statements about God's purpose to reach beyond Israel's boundaries.

To Torah and to rising walls of division, Isaiah 56 says, *Hold on; guess who's coming to worship?* More significantly, guess who's inviting them, welcoming them, making room for them? "Thus says the Lord GOD, who gathers the outcasts of Israel, I will gather others to them besides those already gathered" (Isa. 56:8). The grace of God reveals itself in God's gathering nature. God gathers in worship those nobody expects to belong there. God gathers, in the case of eunuchs, even those whom Torah said did not belong. It is an amazing turn of events. Worship, where place and company do matter, is broken open to the excluded by the grace of God.

Perhaps if this were just one isolated text, one unique experience, we might brush it off as wishful thinking or exaggerated language. But look what happens in the New Testament! Jesus shares table fellowship with every sort of person you wouldn't want sitting in your pew on Sunday. A robber—likely a murderer—named Barabbas is the first person whose place Christ takes in death. The Cross of Christ, according to Paul, demolishes the dividing wall between Jews and Gentiles. Once more, God breaks open the way for a heretofore unwelcomed group to join the community in worship and service of God.

Hospitality toward persons and groups from whom we have been estranged is not easy when it comes to worship. But neither ease, local custom, or personal comfort level is the issue before us. Rather, we face this question: Who gathers, who invites to worship? Isaiah 56 asserts that any joined to God will find themselves welcome by God. "My house shall be called a house of prayers for all peoples" (56:7). If God so graciously welcomes and gathers, what will we do?

> I thank you for your welcome of me, O God, in spite of any offense that might give to some. Help me to welcome others as you would welcome them through me. In Jesus Christ. Amen.

SPIRITUAL EXERCISE

Reread Isaiah 56:1-8 and then verse 3 aloud. Remember a time when you felt such exclusion. How has the grace of God enabled you to deal with that experience? Consider persons in your community, in your church, who might feel separated from others, from God. Pray for God's guidance in how to welcome folks who feel excluded. Offer thanks for the grace that receives you (and them) in Christ.

DAY 6

✦

Finding God
through Serving Neighbor

ISAIAH 58:1-14

Why do we fast, but you do not see?—Isaiah 58:3

A NATIONWIDE EVANGELISTIC CAMPAIGN years ago centered on a well-publicized slogan: "I found it!" Some mused about the phrase being a subtle form of works-righteousness (salvation as *my* doing the finding rather than God's finding me). And if we really are talking about God, is "it" the right reference to deity?

Still, the phrase does capture the widespread and understandable longing of our search for God in life. Hard times come, and we may well wonder where God may be found in tragedy that defies explanation. Good times come, and it may become difficult to find God with so many shiny baubles of prosperity and overabundance to distract and disorient us.

In good times or in bad, the question arises as to where we may best conduct our searching after God. Reading a book like this one forms one such path of inquiry. Other traditional disciplines of spiritual growth offer paths by which persons and communities have sought to discern God's words and ways for life.

Tradition, however, does not always keep up with the God determined to renew and re-create. Take Isaiah 58 and its words about fasting. Fasting, an act of denial, focuses the whole body on spiritual discernment or renewal. As this chapter opens, the people fast, but there is a problem. Fasting isn't working. God isn't responding as God should. People are not finding "it." Something must be wrong—with God!

That's Israel's take on the situation. From God's perspective, fasting doesn't happen in isolation from the rest of life. Feel free to substitute for "fasting" whatever promises encounter with God to you, be it "worship," "spiritual formation," or "Bible study." You can't do what you think will "work" to get God's attention on your life, only to pay no attention to the lives around you. Life is all one piece. Covenant binds you in community. So if you want to find God, Isaiah 58 declares, try the fast God chooses.

Undo injustice. Free people who are captive. Bear burdens that weigh folks down. Share your bread, your home, your clothes. Recognize your kinship with those who need these things and do something about it. Keep sabbath by setting aside self-interest and self-advancement for the sake of One greater than you. That's how Isaiah 58 says the search for God proves fruitful: "Then you shall call, and the LORD will answer" (58:9).

But what about spiritual formation? Spirituality could be defined as awareness of and seeking after encounter with God in daily life. Spiritual formation involves disciplined reflections and practices that focus upon such moments and understandings of encounter. Isaiah 58 simply yet profoundly insists that encounter with God (spirituality) can never be practiced in isolation from community needs. Indeed, the prophet reveals in striking clarity that disciplines of spiritual formation inevitably move in the direction of serving community and neighbor.

Does this mean we abandon our prayer closets and exhaust ourselves solely in social justice ministries in order to be spiritually formed by the God who inspired this text? No. Activism without roots exhausts. Actions without underlying purpose can all too easily be manipulated by those with motives unchecked by covenant. But spirituality that sees the personal journey of faith as its own self-enclosed world runs just as empty and vulnerable to manipulation.

Isaiah 58 acknowledges the importance of searching for and finding God in life. So does Jesus in Matthew 25:31-46. There, one group of people is amazed at the news of having ministered to Christ. They had absolutely no memories of doing any such thing. Jesus' answer sounds suspiciously like Isaiah 58. Bread shared. Hospitality extended. Clothes given. Kinship recognized. "Truly I tell you, just as you did it to one of the least of these who are members of my family, you did it to me" (Matt. 25:40).

Would you like to find God? Find your neighbor. Practice the spirituality of servanthood. For if Isaiah is right, "Then you shall call, and the LORD will answer."

Lead me, O God, that I may find you where you move, and where you would move through me. In Jesus Christ. Amen.

SPIRITUAL EXERCISE

Reread Isaiah 58:6-7. Select at least one "discipline" listed and commit yourself to its practice in a new way. Prayerfully engage in that discipline. Be attentive to those whom you may serve, not as clients but as the bearers of God to you. Be grateful for needs that serve as opportunities. And as you serve, be mindful of your need for sabbath's rest, renewal, and providence.

WEEK SIX

Turning Toward Promise

DAY 1

✦

"I Am for You"

EZEKIEL 36:8-12

See now, I am for you.—Ezekiel 36:9

NEAR THE END of our second year in seminary, my classmates and I took our individual oral examinations before
boards consisting of two professors and a local minister. We had
to pass the orals in order to to proceed to our third and final
year. If we did not pass, one retake was permitted. Failure on
the retake meant dismissal from seminary. Unlike every other
member of my class that year, I failed my orals. Seminary and
ordained ministry had been in my mind and heart since my
senior year in high school. Now I faced the real possibility that
could all change.

I found support and encouragement from classmates, who
sympathized with my plight. But I found empowerment from
two faculty members who counseled me following the first set
of orals and preceding the second. I have long since forgotten
the words they spoke. What I do remember is emerging from
each of those conversations with a strong sense of their advocacy on my behalf. In my heart of hearts, I knew they were
"for" me.

We meet people during the course of our days whom we
know we would want on our side. Sometimes that desire
derives from the power or standing such individuals possess.

Sometimes that desire comes from a spiritual or emotional affinity we feel with them. I recall a time for me when it involved both. Douglas Meeks had taught me to think theologically. Walter Brueggemann had shaped how I listen and respond to the biblical witness. Looking back, if neither had affirmed his advocacy for me, one plausible scenario would have been that my ministry and this book never came to be.

"See now, I am for you." Ezekiel offers this word to a people still in exile, some wondering whether God would ever again turn with grace toward Israel. The prophets and those who took their words to heart perceived the breaches in covenant that broke God's heart and brought them to this state of exile. Still, knowing why you experience separation does not necessarily lead you out of that crisis. It may suggest what to turn from—but *toward* what or whom do you turn? How can deliverance possibly come?

In Ezekiel, God prepares the turning from exile to home, the deliverance from judgment to hope, by declaring this word of advocacy: "I am with you." Consider God drawing close to you in a moment of crisis when you question your very identity, when God's presence falls more on the side of question mark than exclamation point. Hear this One say, "I am for you." Hear those words spoken to a community broken apart by tragedy, torn apart by conflict, or ravaged by injustice: "I am for you." This life-breathing word is intended to be a world-changing word.

At least this word bears that potential. God's advocacy relies to some degree upon its being accepted and then enacted. Sometimes it is too utterly incredible to be accepted. We feel ourselves too unworthy for the likes of God to stand by us. We think we have sinned unlike any other person in all creation. We feel we have passed the point of no return when it comes to grace or hope or renewal. Or, worse yet, we render that judgment upon others. We cannot imagine God to be for the likes of _____. We fill in that blank with those we suppose least deserving of grace in our community, in our church, or in our family. Yet God has a way of speaking those words to the most surprising of folk: Israel in exile, a thief on a cross, society's rejects, and the church's castoffs. "I am for you" whispers grace to corners of life that embarrass us and threaten us—and ultimately include and embrace us.

"I am for you." Remember Moses at the burning bush, where God discloses the divine name? "I am who I am" (Exod. 3:14). That text can also be translated, "I will be who I will be" or "I will cause to be what I will cause to be." Nobody fully understands the definitive meaning of YHWH, except that it relates to the verb *to be.* "I am for you" reminds us that the One to whom Ezekiel refers makes a habit out of bringing new things—and new persons—into being. It is God's name for it is God's nature.

"I am for you." Remember that message when you stand alone, when you stand unworthy, or when you don't stand at all. "I am for you."

> *"I am for you." How many times do you have to say those words to me, O God, before I trust them? How many times must you say those words to others before I accept them? Help me to be for you. Amen.*

SPIRITUAL EXERCISE

Reread Ezekiel 36:8-12. Read aloud, "I am for you" several times. The first time, say your name after those words. Reflect on times when you have sensed God's advocacy for you. The second time, say the name of your faith community after those words. In your journal, make note of how those words might deepen that community's trust and service. The third time, say the name of a group in your community or the world in desperate need of advocacy. Consider one way in which you might be a partner of God's advocacy for them in this coming week. Be that advocate.

DAY 2

✦

Maranatha!

EZEKIEL 40:1-2; 43:1-5

The glory of the LORD filled the temple.—Ezekiel 43:5

MARANATHA. DO YOU recognize the word? If you do, chances are you know it from the Christian music group called Maranatha or a congregation by that name. *Maranatha* comes from the Semitic language Aramaic, most likely Jesus' native tongue. It means "Our Lord, come" or "Our Lord will come." *Maranatha* served in the early church—and in that word's recent revival—to express fervent hope in and a prayer for Jesus' imminent return. The one appearance of *maranatha* in scripture comes at the end of Paul's first letter to the Corinthians. There the benediction of Christ's grace and Paul's love goes prefaced by "Our Lord, come!"—Maranatha!

The theme of God's coming is not limited to speculations about rapture or to Advent's cyclical reminder of God's incarnation in the Bethlehem birth. Israel's prophets understood both judgment and hope to be consequences of God's coming. Today's text from Ezekiel offers an insightful word about a coming that will undo a leaving.

Recall Ezekiel's earlier vision of judgment, when the glory of God mounts on wings and leaves the Temple and city (10:9-22; 11:22-25). God's presence headed east, where Ezekiel and others already in exile awaited word of Jerusalem's final destruction. God's departure from the city envisioned by the prophet brought an end to false hopes. Hope and restoration would await God's purposes—and God's coming.

Ezekiel 43:1-5 stands in the midst of a vision that began with chapter 40 and runs through chapter 48. The whole vision depicts in extraordinary detail a restored Temple and land. The significance of all those mundane details of measurement, structure, chambers, gates, and doors may escape us today. After all, we can worship God anywhere, in any setting.

Ezekiel, however, attends to the meanings attached to sacred space. In elaborating the minutiae, Ezekiel intends to convey the total restoration of what had fallen prey to abuse and misuse. The Temple once fled by God for breach of covenant will be restored, so that God may once again return to the heart of Israel's life. Ezekiel narrates God's dramatic reentry into Jerusalem and the Temple. The details of the glory of God coming from the east hearken back to the direction where God's presence had gone: with the people, into exile. The promised return from exile finds anticipation in God's returning from that same direction. The same way in which judgment had fallen, hope returns. Our God comes. Maranatha!

Reading Ezekiel 43, one might think the deal completed and God's return imminent and obvious. Such thinking overlooks one crucial detail at the vision's beginning: "In the twenty-fifth year of our exile . . ." (40:1). Ezekiel had gone with the first wave of Jews into exile in 597 BCE. The twenty-fifth year would place this vision in 572 BCE. When did exile end, at least for those who risked leaving the certainties and securities of life in Babylon? 538 BCE. For thirty plus years, Ezekiel's vision of exile's ending and God's coming remained a matter of faith rather than sight. Hope rather than knowledge.

Promise rather than certainty. Have you ever hoped in something or someone for thirty years and more? Have you ever waited so long you started to wonder why? Maranatha?

Turning toward promise, even the promise of God's coming, does not instantly and completely transform the landscape of the world or one's life. Turning toward promise simply yet profoundly keeps eyes and spirits focused on where and in whom this world finds its origin and destiny. Even in those places where God's presence seems absent for the moment, God's coming promises restoration.

In Ezekiel's vision, God transported him to Jerusalem. There Ezekiel looked to the east. Previously it had been the direction in which God left the city in judgment. When Ezekiel looked east, he saw hope in the return of Holy Presence. Paul looked to the end of this age, marked by more than its share of sufferings and promises delayed. He saw hope in "a plan for the fullness of time, to gather up all things in [Christ], things in heaven and things on earth" (Eph. 1:10).

Where we look reveals our hope. What we hope generates our discipleship. Maranatha!

> *Do not give up on our coming to you nor let us give up on your coming to us in the face of a stranger in need or in the hope of a promise unfulfilled. Our Lord, come! Maranatha! Amen.*

SPIRITUAL EXERCISE

In your journal, reflect on some promise or hope you have long held—and still hold, though its fulfillment remains to be seen. What aspect of that promise or hope has sustained you? What role has God or faith played in this vigil? Pray for faithfulness. Pray for God's coming. Pray for hope for you, for others.

DAY 3

✦

New Wineskins

JEREMIAH 23:5-8

And this is the name by which he will be called: "The LORD is our righteousness."—Jeremiah 23:6

MATTHEW 9:17 AND Mark 2:22 record a proverb Jesus told about the folly of pouring new wine into old wineskins. New wine, whose aging creates expanding gases, would burst older skins no longer able to stretch. New skins, still pliable, are needed to keep pace with the fermentation occurring within. The context of Jesus' words involved a question on fasting, a discipline of piety that some judged Jesus' disciples were ignoring. Jesus' proverb implies that new ways of not only expressing piety but also practicing faith loom on the horizon.

Jeremiah 21–22 announced the unhappy news of God's judgment against the political leaders of a besieged Jerusalem. Jeremiah 22:13-17 asserts the core reasons for God's opposing the current royal house: A lack of righteousness and justice condemn this dynastic line. Things will never be as they were again. Of that truth Jeremiah provides devastating witness. But the end of life as it was does not mean the end of hope, unless hope rests only in the status quo.

Jeremiah 23:5-8 interrupts the narrative of doom with an outburst of hope. The prophet pours out promise as a vintner might fill skins with new wine. Like new wine fermenting into fine wine, so promise is intended to transform into hope. But fermentation—or transformation—can be dangerous if you don't have a pliable vessel capable of expanding. For Jeremiah, old names and even old theological assertions cannot adequately contain what God promises to do. "The LORD is our righteousness" announces the name of the promised king who will execute justice. In a play on words, the name of Judah's current king, who has failed to do justice, is Zedekiah (in Hebrew, "Yahweh is righteous"). His claim to justice is in name only: The one promised of God in verse 6 will execute justice in word and deed. To return to the metaphor of new wine and promise, life grown brittle through injustice cannot bear God's expansive promises that produce hope.

What God is about to do, even more extraordinarily, demands a new understanding of deliverance. The Exodus in Judaism parallels the Cross in Christianity. It is the formative act of God's deliverance in Judaism's identity. Yet God's promised redemption summons for Jeremiah a need to speak of an even greater act of deliverance than Exodus (23:7-8). The power and scandal of Jeremiah's words here are comparable to a Christian theologian's pointing to an act of deliverance greater than the Cross. Unimaginable, one would think.

Precisely. For Jeremiah, God's promises summon a new imagination of faith. Speaking of what God will do cannot be exhausted by trotting out ancient formulas. Pointing to the present or the past cannot adequately illuminate God's future. Turning toward promise invites us to stretch our faith and service, our community and spiritual disciplines, beyond what we might once have considered possible. Certainly it invites us to move beyond what society dictates as "practical" or "normative." We are heirs, we are adherents, of words and hopes that defy convention. What God has done, however miraculous, does not tell the whole story of what God may yet do. Perhaps John Robinson captured a piece of that spirit in his parting words to the Pilgrims about to set sail for the New World. Robinson encouraged them to trust the God who "hath yet more lighte to breake forth from his worde."

Seeking more light from the biblical word forms but one aspect of living with faithful imagination. Practice disciplines of prayer that encourage listening. When prayer is mostly or solely what we bring to God, we may have difficulty hearing what God might convey beyond what we already "know" to be our hopes and petitions. Practice disciplines of community that invoke the future as much as the present or past in decision making. Once we trust that the future belongs to God, we can let go of the sometimes oppressive need to maintain current (or past) definitions of identity and mission. For who we are and what we do, now or in the past, does not limit all that God would ever make of us as persons or as congregations.

Above all else, practice the discipline of remaining open to God's promissory ways. According to Ecclesiastes' world-wise but spirit-wearying declaration, "What has been is what will be, and what has been done is what will be done; there is nothing new under the sun" (1:9). Sooner or later, faith faces a choice of living according to the rigid stoicism of Ecclesiastes or the future-opening promises of prophets like Jeremiah.

So how choose you?

> *Teach me, in Christ, the gift of hope: born in wonder and surprise, incarnate in fresh acts of deliverance unimagined before. And in such hope, O God, stretch my faith to fit your promise. Amen.*

SPIRITUAL EXERCISE

Reread Jeremiah 23:7–8. Imagine how those words might have sounded to those for whom the Exodus defined faith. In your journal, write the words of verse 7 and the beginning of 8 through "As the LORD lives who." In the space following, write how you or your community has experienced God's deliverance. Reflect on how that has changed you and others.

DAY 4

Grieving and Remembrance

JEREMIAH 31:15-20

I still remember him.—Jeremiah 31:20

A S A PASTOR, I have attended to grievings of all manner. I buried a young man at whose marriage I had officiated. He died the year following his marriage in the same hospital room where his wife had rested after giving birth to their first child. I baptized a drowned little boy who simply looked asleep in his mother's cradling arms. I interred the ashes of a good friend of our son, a bright star extinguished by a single bad choice. Those persons who grieved these deaths, myself included, have never been the same since.

That is as it should be.

Grief does change us. Loss cries out for expression. And woe to those who would deny or minimize its expression. In searching for an adequate depiction of the grief heaped on by exile, Jeremiah reaches deep into his tradition. He hears the voice of a mother weeping. Rachel. Rachel died in childbirth (Gen. 35:16-20), an occasion then and now of extraordinary grief. Jeremiah invokes this figure of grief to lament her children, the people of Israel in exile, who are no more.

But what has grief to do with turning toward promise?

Life as it is cannot be denied or recast to suit our wishes. Grieving for what and who have been but are no longer belongs just as much to moving forward and finding renewal as asserting cause to hope. Indeed, the strength and vision to speak hope in the face of grief comes only after acknowledging and confronting the reality of what has come to pass.

Movement toward the future paradoxically involves the act of remembrance. In response to a plea in Jeremiah's text raised by "Ephraim"(a frequent synonym for Israel), God engages in a bit of conflicted reflection. Ephraim's words ("I repented") and God's candidness ("as often as I speak against him") leave no doubt that just cause for grief exists. Yet God's grief for the one who has turned away and bears disgrace evokes, "I still remember him." Such remembrance moves God deeply. Grief changes God's disposition from judgment to mercy. The genesis of such change comes in grief brought to remembrance.

Rachel weeps, and God responds. Ephraim grieves dead-end ways, and God remembers.

When God remembers in scripture, life happens. God remembers Noah and all the animals; remembrance blows winds and subsides waters (Gen. 8:1 ff). God remembers the covenant when Israel languishes in Egypt; deliverance comes. So now in Jeremiah, the means of hope and the encouragement for turning toward promise come in God's remembering.

Jeremiah's insights translate into key considerations for our own spiritual journey toward promise. To begin with, we must be prepared to grieve. Look around at this world. If we do not grieve, we may have grown too numb. Affluence numbs by cushioning us from what others endure. Despair numbs by convincing us nothing ever truly changes. Apathy numbs by fostering the impression we have no responsibility to be our brothers' and sisters' keepers. Numbness dulls our ability to feel, to empathize, to have *com*passion—whose literal meaning is to "suffer with." Contrary to the practice of medicating persons through bereavement, grief leads to healing and wholeness precisely because it brings our feelings, our pain, to the surface.

Rachel weeps for her children; Ephraim grieves a deadening past; and new life begins to emerge.

We must be prepared to remember in life-giving ways. To be sure, remembrance can become oppressive: remembrance as holding grudges, as never forgetting wrongs. But remembrance can be redemptive. God remembers more than what has been spoken against Ephraim. God remembers him as the dear child, the delight, the one toward whom God is deeply moved and merciful. It is easier to remember the potential of persons, even with all their mistakes and missteps, if we remember the grace of God for us and for all.

Know that God remembers you and delights in you. Trust that God seeks for you such turning toward promise that brings hope, grace, and empowerment.

> *Holy God, trouble me and grace me with grief so that I may feel and see what needs to be buried. Trouble me and grace me with remembrance so that I may feel and see hope raised up in you. Amen.*

SPIRITUAL EXERCISE

Read Jeremiah 31:15-20. In your journal, reflect on grieving for someone or something no more in your life. Be aware that God remembers you as the child in whom God delights. Be at prayer for a grieving that opens you to new life, a remembrance that brings you into God's presence, and a hope that flows out of your identity as God's beloved child.

DAY 5
+

Raising Jubilee

ISAIAH 61:1-3

The spirit of the Lord GOD is upon me . . . to proclaim the
year of the LORD'S favor.—Isaiah 61:1-2

THE SOVEREIGN REALM of God may be compared to a woman who journeys to her grandmother's birthplace. After gaining permission of the home's owner, she tours the house. All is as she remembered. The richly grained kitchen cabinets. The wardrobe in her grandmother's bedroom where the woman used to hide as a child. The stone fireplace and book-laden shelves in the library. When she opens the doors to a parlor, however, she lets out a gasp. A huge boulder dominates the room. Looking outside, she can see the path it cleared when it rolled down the cliff behind the house and smashed through the wall. The wall and windows have been fixed, and even the flooring around the boulder has been refinished, but the boulder stands untouched. At dinner that evening, she watches as the current family's members bring dishes and food from the kitchen to the dining room and back again, moving past the boulder as if it does not exist. Baffled, she asks how they could possibly ignore this enormous rock in their midst. "Ignoring it is hard enough," comes the answer, "but doing something about it would be even harder."

Leviticus 25 details the requirements for the Year of Jubilee. Every fiftieth year, at the end of the seventh of seven sabbath-year cycles, the land was to lie fallow; debts were to be forgiven; land ownership was to be restored to its original line of inheritance; and slaves were to be freed. This Jubilee intended to put into practice God's claim as Israel's "Redeemer," whose redemption involved not only spiritual but social transformation.

Writing in his book *Theology of the Old Testament*, Walter Brueggemann notes the question he is asked most frequently about any command in the Old Testament: "There is no evidence, is there, that Israel ever in fact implemented this command [jubilee]?" For all practical purposes, the radical reversals called for by Jubilee went ignored by the community. Jubilee very much resembles the boulder in the parable. Its presence in the Hebrew scriptures is hard to ignore, but apparently doing something about it would have been even harder.

So Jubilee went ignored—but not forgotten.

In the recital of Isaiah 61:1-3, the one anointed and sent by God will, among other things, "proclaim the year of the LORD's favor." That is, God's anointed will declare a Jubilee. In the Levitical legislation, Jubilee aimed at rectifying imbalances suffered by those on society's margins: the indebted, the disinherited, the wearied. Listen to those for whom Isaiah's Jubilee brings respite: the oppressed, brokenhearted, captive, prisoners, mourners. To such persons Isaiah 61 bears words of hope by remembering the long-unfulfilled promise of Leviticus 25.

But how exactly does one turn toward such promise when it appears for all practical purposes to have been a promise never even attempted? The verbs of Isaiah 61 provide a clue. Bring good news. Bind up. Proclaim liberty. Comfort. Provide for. The text does not ask belief in the promise of Jubilee. The text does not prescribe a passive expectancy that all good things will come to those who wait. The verbs invite action, Jubilee set to word and deed.

Do we then dismiss Isaiah 61 as a well-intentioned albeit utopian dream that fell short of the Jerusalem that finally did emerge from exile and restoration? Consider the fourth chapter of Luke. Jesus prepares to preach his inaugural sermon in the hometown synagogue of Nazareth. He unrolls a scroll and reads Isaiah 61:1-2, concluding with "the year of the LORD'S favor." Immediately Jesus says, "Today this scripture has been fulfilled in your hearing" (Luke 4:21).

Jubilee inaugurates the ministry of Jesus Christ. And who are we but the body of Christ? And what is our mission but that of the One we follow, whose name we bear, whose Spirit anoints us, whose Jubilee we announce?

Spiritual formation does not always move us inward into ever-deepening reflections on our personal faith journeys. To be formed by God's Spirit can also entail being pushed outward for the sake of others for the sake of God's mission. Isaiah 61 testifies to a Spirit whose anointing presence begets sending, action, and witness, all for the sake of raising Jubilee out of the shadows. Whether Israel ever fully enacted this word begs the text's enduring question: How will this word, how will this Spirit, form and send us?

The spirit of the Lord is upon . . . you! To bring good news. To bind up brokenhearted ones. To proclaim liberty to captives and release to prisoners. To provide for those who mourn. To proclaim Christ's Jubilee. So God sends those formed by God's Spirit. So God sends you.

> *Form me in your image, O God, and form me in your call,*
> *so that in finding your Spirit within me, I may serve your*
> *Christ beyond me, in the news and acts of your Jubilee.*
> *Amen.*

SPIRITUAL EXERCISE

Read Isaiah 61:1-3 aloud, substituting your name for every occurrence of "me" in the text. Reflect in your journal on what it means for you to be "anointed" by Spirit and sent by God. Read the text a second time, substituting the name of your congregation for occurrences of "me." Pray for the mission of your congregation and your involvement within it.

DAY 6

✦

Second Wind

ISAIAH 65:17-25

For I am about to create new heavens and a new earth; the former things shall not be remembered or come to mind.—Isaiah 65:17

IN SEPTEMBER OF 1990, I trudged up a ridge in Mount Rainier National Park along with our former exchange student from Germany. The destination, decided upon the night before, was the ice caves at the headwaters of the Paradise River. Although I had been to Mount Rainier numerous times and even worked there one summer, the ice caves remained one place I had never visited. Most years, snowpack blocked entrance to the point where the river emerges from under the glacier. The past winter had been dry, however, and the caves were accessible.

That day two obstacles stood between us and the caves: the steep switchbacks and the will to press forward. For seasoned hikers like my companion, Frank, neither posed a problem. For people like me, both loomed large. Physical fatigue begets mental fatigue, and vice versa. Still, about two and a half hours after setting out, both of us stepped inside the hollowed tube under the glacier. Sunlight refracted through the ice above, illumining the tunnel with an eerie blue light. I have never been anywhere like it before or since.

Second wind made it possible for me to stand at that opening. I don't know its medical explanation, but breath once hot and labored eases and refreshes. Just when it seems legs can't take one more step or bear one more switchback, off they go. Second wind kicks in.

My experiences with second wind convince me that it is not purely physical in origin or effect. If Frank hadn't been with me that day or if I had been out for a hike with no particular goal, I suspect I would have turned back. Second wind doesn't seem to come to those intending to go only until they're tired. It comes when a purpose pulls you through low times, beyond tiredness. Second wind enables you to reach the sought-after higher ground, whether figurative or literal.

Isaiah 65 envisions God's promise of new heavens and a new earth. It heralds a time when potential never fails to reach fruition, a place where none shall "hurt or destroy on all my holy mountain." It is a high-soaring text, filled with the imagery of what God intends for this creation and the future. It is also a text about second wind.

Many who study the book of Isaiah understand chapters 55 onward to address the Israelites who have returned from exile in Babylon to rebuild Jerusalem. Immense difficulties face the returnees. Mount Zion, Jerusalem's site, lies in rubble. Other peoples have drifted into the lands and towns of those led away in exile. Strangers inhabit houses of past generations. Newcomers harvest vineyards and groves planted by the exiles' ancestors. In something akin to Jacob's usurping the blessing of Esau, Israel's children come home to find others enjoying the birthright. No doubt those returning from exile shed abundant tears over what has become of the land and its former blessings, not to mention the future.

Into this wearying situation, Isaiah 65 speaks a word of second wind. Its vision intends to invigorate folks facing the enormous task of rebuilding city and Temple with the assurance of the future God intends. But notice: No snap of the divine fingers suddenly lifts walls into place and erects a sanctuary as Israel stands amazed but idle. Second wind is not given so you can watch from the sidelines in greater ease. Second wind comes to those who have a ways to go yet, to those still immersed in the journey. Second wind breathes fresh life and energy into persons and communities who look ahead and see even more switchbacks and ridges to ascend.

For that reason, Isaiah 65 speaks to us. You and I both know the promised new heavens and earth aren't quite here yet. The sound of weeping still echoes far too frequently. The grief known by parents and families with SIDS victims reminds us some infants still live but a few days. The devastation wrought by Alzheimer's disease robs old persons, and some not so old, of living out their lifetimes. Too many people continue to build and plant for subsistence wages, only to have others inhabit and prosper as a result of economic and trade inequities.

That the world confronts us with such trying realities becomes, for some, cause to throw hands in the air and lament how things are headed to hell in a handbasket. Others find in such circumstances a compelling call to service. Eyes wide open to the world and its inequities may take our breath away. When that happens, Isaiah 65 offers us second wind. The future does not belong to what impoverishes and breeds despair. The future belongs to the Holy One who will bring new heavens and earth and with them new justice and compassion. In that hope comes second breath for those who trust and then act.

It is right and fitting to draw this book to a conclusion with Isaiah's vision. The transformation sought by the prophets always finds motivation in Who stands at the end of history and therefore also in its midst. The spiritual re-formation we seek likewise finds its motive and its possibility in the God who would move us into new life. Spiritual disciplines do not merely intend to make of us more inwardly discerning persons. At their best, these disciplines would shape us into persons and communities ever more faithful, enlivened, empowered, and encouraged to step into this world and these days and say: *This is not all there is! This is not all there shall be!*

What enables us to risk such affirmations? God is about to create new heavens and a new earth! So live in the hope of God's sovereign realm. Trust in the presence of God's empowering Spirit. Serve in the example of Christ's gracious love.

Peace be with you on this journey. And may God grant you second wind as you strive toward that holy mountain where none shall hurt or destroy. The new creation will come. The promises can be trusted. Thanks be to God!

> *I rejoice in your creation, Holy God, Giver of all life—and even more I rejoice in your new creation, Coming Redeemer, Assurance of all hope. Keep my eyes and my feet on your way. Amen.*

SPIRITUAL EXERCISE

Read Isaiah 65:17-25 aloud, pausing after each verse. In that pause, remember someone for whom those particular words speak hope. Offer a brief prayer. Continue. At the end, reread those verses with your own life in mind. Give thanks for the hope this text brings to you—and pray for courage in the service and witness to which you hear these words calling you.

LEADER'S GUIDE

Introduction

THESE SUGGESTED SESSION outlines have been developed to aid those who choose to use *Turn Toward Promise* as a group study resource. These sessions have been included here rather than published in a separate volume to make it easier to involve more than one person in planning and leading the sessions.

The study is intended to run over the course of a six-week period. It will be critical for participants in the group to read the material to be covered (and do the accompanying Spiritual Exercises) in the week *prior* to the meeting. So in your planning, make sure participants have the books at least one week ahead of the first session, with instructions to do the reading and exercises for Week 1. You might have an informal group meeting the week prior to the first session. At that meeting you could distribute the materials, walk through the structure of the book, do some initial community building, and give instructions about the readings and exercises to be done each week. If you use this study during Lent—and there are additional suggestions in the session guides for doing so—plan your weekly gatherings so that they do not conflict with traditional or special services your church may offer during that season. Sessions have been planned to take between forty-five minutes and an hour.

Each session consists of five parts:

PREPARATION includes suggestions not only for readying the room and gathering needed materials but for your own spiritual preparations as leader.

OPENING provides suggestions for activities, including an opening prayer that will help introduce the theme in activities or discussion.

INSIGHTS provides an intentional time each week for participants to reflect on the readings and Spiritual Exercises of the past week. Do not gloss over or rush through this time. It may well present unexpected perspectives or thought-provoking considerations not anticipated in the session guide but nonetheless important to be raised within the group.

EXPLORATIONS provides time and activities to delve deeper into one or more aspects of the week's theme. For those who have more than one hour to devote to each session, the experiences in Explorations (as well as Insights) could easily be expanded.

CLOSING offers opportunities to summarize and reflect on the group experience, make any assignments for the following week, and close with a liturgical act.

If you are limited to forty-five minutes for meeting time, use the following guide:

Opening	10 minutes
Insights	15 minutes
Exploration	15 minutes
Closing	5 minutes

If you have more time available (an hour to an hour and a half), the additional time will allow you to enter more deeply into the Insights and Exploration segments. Certainly there may be times when, due to energy around a discussion or depth of participant involvement, a group may choose to dwell longer on some parts of the plan. Be open to follow the group's movement and the Spirit's leading as you make decisions about how to proceed.

Two sessions use Reflection Guides for individuals to fill out during the time together. Those sessions may need to be extended. Looking ahead at the session plan and keeping your particular group in mind will also help you anticipate situations that may need special attention or extended time.

Thank you for your leadership in these sessions—and for letting these experiences transform you even as they offer opportunities of transformation for all who will be taking part.

SESSION PLAN
FOR WEEK ONE

Confronting a New Reality

PREPARATION

Preparing Yourself Spiritually

Read Week 1 of *Turn Toward Promise*. Do each of the daily Spiritual Exercises. As you approach this week, consider times when you have had to look at the reality of your life in a new way. What helped you to assess your situation? As suggested in "Before You Begin," keep a journal based on your reflections upon the readings and exercises. Maintain a discipline of daily prayer that grows out of the readings and exercises. Review this session guide early in the week to allow adequate time for preparation. Pray for each participant you expect to come to the session (and any who may come unexpectedly), and pray for God's Spirit to lead you in your service as group leader.

Offer this or a similar prayer before leading this session:

> *God, open my eyes to see you, to see the persons in this group, to see this world in new ways. And by your Spirit, help me to live in faith and trust. In Jesus Christ. Amen.*

Preparing the Room and Materials

Place a candle and an open Bible on a small table to use as a worship center. Have a lighter or matches available. Post pictures or headlines that depict new situations confronting individuals and your faith community. Ideally the items displayed should reflect not only "welcomed" additions (birth of a child, new program at church, new community asset) but some that are troubling (local, international, or personal crises).

Preparing to Focus

This session focuses on our need to acknowledge new realities that may surprise or challenge us in the course of our lives and spiritual development. God does not always (or often!) leave us as or where we are. This week's texts from Israel's prophets and the readings underscore that movement through which God seeks to transform our lives as individuals and communities.

OPENING

- Greet people by name as they enter the gathering space. When all have arrived, welcome persons to this series of group experiences based on *Turn Toward Promise*. Underscore how keeping up with the daily readings, Spiritual Exercises, and journal work will enable them to experience fully this opportunity for spiritual formation.

- Ask individuals to reflect silently on these questions:

  What new situation have you faced in your life during the past year? Looking back, where did you discern God in that experience or in its outcome?

After a time of quiet reflection, invite individuals who are willing to say a few words about their thoughts. Form groups of three or four persons to do this sharing. Next, invite persons to reflect on and respond to the same questions in the context of your faith community.

> LENTEN EMPHASIS: Call to mind how Lent serves as a time
> for confronting realities, old and new, in our lives. Point out
> the intent of Lent's traditional discipline of "giving up" a
> food or activity, which is to promote focused examination
> of what we do in our lives, and why, relative to Jesus' call to
> discipleship and bearing our own cross. Invite conversation
> in the group about how Lent might bring fresh insights or
> discipline to those experiences people recalled in the pre-
> vious activity. What has the cross to do with them?

- Call on one person to light the candle as a visible reminder
  that you gather in God's presence, seeking God's light for
  your lives.

- Offer this or a similar prayer:

  *God of history, God of community, God who comes to us
  in each new and changing circumstance, God who opens
  yourself to us in ways we do not always perceive or would
  not always choose: Draw near to us now. Give us hearts
  and minds, words and actions, open to you. Give us energy
  and faith for this journey we make with one another in
  company with you. In Jesus Christ. Amen.*

INSIGHTS

- Ask the group members to identify their experience of
  God's presence and word in their lives this past week generated through the daily readings and exercises.

  – Give participants a moment to look over their journals.
    Then ask individuals to share what spoke most deeply to
    them. Encourage listening that seeks to discern the pres-
    ence and movement of God in each person's insights. (If
    you have a large group—over twelve persons—you may

wish to form small groups for this sharing in order to allow deeper conversations.)

— Offer your response to this week's readings and exercises if needed to stimulate conversation.

— After everyone has spoken, suggest that the group identify patterns or themes that have emerged. If you formed small groups, preface this step with a report from each group summarizing its sharing.

LENTEN EMPHASIS: Ask participants to draw parallels between these responses and themes to the season of Lent. Consider how the experiences and exercises recounted above relate to persons' understandings of Lent as a time of spiritual discipline and reformation.

EXPLORATIONS

The size of your group will determine how you pursue the following exploration. You need at least three persons to work together as a group for any of these activities. If you have a small group, do not try to cover all six readings. Focus on two or three.

• Form small groups of no less than three persons—and no more than six groups. Have each group select one of the daily readings from this week (you may need to assign or at least oversee the selections, so that groups do not duplicate their selections).

• Instruct each group to develop a presentation (skit, pantomime with reader, role play, or other) based on that reading's emphasis. The point is to set these presentations in one of the "new realities" faced by individuals or your congregation as identified in the opening activity.

- Allow adequate time for planning and then the presentations themselves (ten minutes if you have a forty-five-minute session; longer if time is available).

- After each presentation, allow time for brief observations.

- When the presentations are completed, invite discussion on the theme of confronting new realities that come to us, and sometimes are forced on us. Ask how the presentations portrayed the role and presence of God in those situations. What does faithfulness entail and not entail in such times and places? Invite participants to identify the importance of experiences like these in spiritual formation.

LENTEN EMPHASIS: The Lenten journey took the first disciples to places they would not have chosen on their own. New realities of a suffering Messiah and costly discipleship came to the forefront. Identify how the presentations touched on such Lenten themes and how "following Christ" can at times be a difficult discipline to accept.

CLOSING

- Gather persons in a circle around the worship center and join hands. Silently look at the pictures or headlines you have displayed. Affirm that to be alive is to confront change—sometimes welcomed, sometimes not. Invite brief comments on what persons will carry with them from this session, especially about discerning God in the midst of crisis or change.

- Lead the group in a closing sentence prayer. Explain that each person around the circle will have opportunity to offer a brief prayer. If an individual does not wish to pray aloud, he or she simply squeezes the hand of the person to the left. Begin by offering your sentence prayer and let the prayer move around the circle.

- At the prayer's end, offer this or another benediction:

  Go from this place, knowing you journey with God; offer grace to others, as you find grace in Christ; be at peace, as you dwell in the peace of the Spirit of God.

- Make any necessary announcements. Remind everyone to read daily in Week 2 and to do the related exercises and journal entries.

SESSION PLAN
FOR WEEK TWO

Casting Off Illusions

PREPARATION

Preparing Yourself Spiritually

Read Week 2 of *Turn Toward Promise*. Do each of the daily Spiritual Exercises. As you prepare for this week, reflect on illusions you have had to come to grips with in your own life and relationships as well as in the life of your community or church. What in your faith helped you to see the truth in such situations and to give up false impressions? As suggested in "Before You Begin," keep a journal based on your reflections upon the readings and experiences of the exercises. Maintain a discipline of daily prayer that grows out of the readings and exercises. Review this session guide early in the week to allow adequate time for preparation of its activities. Pray for each participant you expect to be there (and those who may come unexpectedly), and pray for God's Spirit to lead you in your service as group leader.

Offer this or a similar prayer before leading this session:

> *Lead me, O God, to truth. Help me not to settle for only what I hope is true or trustworthy. Guide us together in this session into such truth. In Jesus Christ. Amen.*

Preparing the Room and Materials

Gather and display materials that illustrate or create illusions. For example, mirrors that distort reflected images, darkly tinted glasses or colored panes of glass (no sharp edges, please), inaccurate headlines ("Dewey Defeats Truman"), books or posters on sleight-of-hand tricks. Also, set aside a small table for a worship center that participants will easily view. Place a candle on it and have matches or a lighter to use. Alongside the candle place a Bible open to Isaiah, with bookmarks placed in Jeremiah and Ezekiel.

Preparing to Focus

In this session you will explore the importance of setting aside illusions about life and faith and community. The lens through which to focus on illusion and reality is Israel's confrontation with the reality of her situation.

OPENING

• Greet participants by name as they enter. Make sure folks are introduced to one another if some are unknown to others. During this gathering time, suggest that people browse the materials you have gathered and displayed. Without explaining at this point what the items represent, let people reflect on what they have in common and how they might relate to this session.

• Have individuals pair off and ask the partners to tell each other three things about themselves probably unknown by others in the group. One of those "facts" should be made up. When the group comes back together, each person introduces his or her partner by sharing those three identity pieces. Have the introducer guess which fact is fiction (and, if time allows, invite the group to guess as well) before asking the partner to reveal the "illusion."

• Invite participants who wish to offer words about or reactions to the materials on display. Affirm what each individual sees, while moving the conversation to matters of illusion and reality. Explain that this session will explore how confronting illusion is an important foundational step in spiritual formation and reformation, a step discerned in the readings from these prophets.

> LENTEN EMPHASIS: Relate how Lent has traditionally been a time for persons in the church to reflect on spiritual values and priorities, which is in one sense a movement to center our lives on what faith and life truly is rather than what it merely "appears" to be.

• Call on one person to light the candle as a visible reminder during this and other sessions that you gather in God's presence, seeking God's light for your lives.

• Offer this or a similar prayer:

> *God of truth, God of light, you who move among us even now: Be present in our words to one another, be present in silence kept, be present in scripture, be present in thought. Hold up to us the truth of our lives, even as you hold us in the truth of your grace. In Jesus Christ. Amen.*

INSIGHTS

• Ask the group members to identify their experience of God's presence and word in their lives this past week generated through the daily readings and exercises.

- Give participants a moment to look over their journals. Then ask individuals to share what spoke most deeply to them. Encourage listening that seeks to discern the presence and movement of God in each person's insights.

- If you have a large group (over twelve persons), you may wish to form small groups for this sharing in order to allow deeper conversations.

- Offer your response to this week's readings and exercises if needed to stimulate conversation.

- After everyone has spoken, invite the group to identify patterns or themes that have emerged. If you formed small groups, preface this with a report from each group that summarizes the sharing that took place within the group.

LENTEN EMPHASIS: Ask participants to draw parallels between these responses and themes to the season of Lent. Consider how the experiences and exercises recounted above relate to persons' understandings of Lent as a time of spiritual discipline and reformation.

EXPLORATIONS

- Explore how these passages invite the individuals in your group (yourself included) to cast aside illusions about life or faith in order to experience spiritual reformation.

  - Have persons turn to the Reflection Guide on page 171. Invite them to choose two of the sets of verses and questions to use for personal reflection.

– Direct individuals to find a quiet space in the room or another location to work alone. Suggest that they write responses to the questions in their journals.

– Gather persons together after an appropriate and adequate time of working alone (seven minutes for a forty-five-minute session; ten minutes if more time is available). Invite individuals to respond to this exercise: its value, its challenge, its drawing them into the presence of God and the discipline of spiritual reformation.

LENTEN EMPHASIS: Remind participants how Lent stands as a journey that leads to Jerusalem, a journey that the first disciples found difficult precisely because it forced them to reconsider assumptions about God and the meaning of faithfulness. Casting aside illusions was just as much a part of their experience as it was Isaiah's challenge to Israel—and to us. Discuss how "journey" connects with the reflections on and discussions stemming from the Reflection Guide.

CLOSING

• Allow a time for individuals to offer brief responses to this gathering. Helpful questions might include:

What especially touched your heart and mind?
When did you feel yourself in the presence of God?

• Gather persons around the worship center, standing or sitting. Invite them to focus on the light of the candle and the opened Bible and consider what lingers with them from this gathering. Invite silent reflection on what they have experienced as light—brought from these prophets and from one another—that dispels illusions and points them toward God.

- Explain that you will be asking persons to speak a sentence or two based on those reflections of what serves as light for them. After each person's sharing, the group responds:

  For the light you bring to help us see, we give you thanks, O God.

  Have persons repeat this response two or three times to become familiar with it.

- Carry out the "litany"; you may wish to go first to get the prayer activity rolling.

- Remind everyone to read daily in Week 3 and to do the related Spiritual Exercises and journal entries. Make announcements about the next meeting (time, place) and other matters for the common good.

- Offer this or another benediction:

  Go from this place, knowing you journey with God; offer grace to others, as you find grace in Christ; be at peace, as you dwell in the peace of the very Spirit of God.

REFLECTiON GUiDE

"What to me is the multitude of your sacrifices? . . . cease to do evil, learn to do good."—Isaiah 1:11,16-17

- What "fills" my faith without really bringing me any closer to God?

- What do I need to learn to do during this season of Lent?

"A shoot shall come out from the stump of Jesse, and a branch shall grow out of his roots."—Isaiah 11:1

- What signs of spiritual growth do I see in places that seemed lifeless or buried?

- What doors do I need to close in order to open my spirit to God's fresh appearing?

"Here you are, trusting in deceptive words to no avail."—Jeremiah 7:8

- What "deceptive words" today mislead people—mislead you—about God's purposes?

- What would help you act more justly toward others and faithful toward God?

"If in a safe land you fall down, how will you fare in the thickets of the Jordan?"—Jeremiah 12:5

- What relatively minor hurdles have frustrated your relationship with God?

- How do you prepare yourself spiritually for confronting life's major tests?

"You are not sent to a people of obscure speech and difficult language."—Ezekiel 3:5

- Where have you struggled to accept or even hear words that portended change for you?

- What creates stubbornness in your life and spiritual journey?

"'Every vision comes to nothing' . . . None of my words will be delayed any longer."—Ezekiel 12:22, 28

- What in your spiritual life would you "put off for another day"? Why?

- What is God working on in you? in your faith community?

SESSION PLAN
FOR WEEK THREE

Speaking Truth to Power

PREPARATION

Preparing Yourself Spiritually

Read Week 3 of *Turn Toward Promise*. Do each of the daily Spiritual Exercises. As you ready yourself for this session, reflect on what "speaking truth to power" means to you? What experiences or examples illustrate that meaning? Record these thoughts in your journal. As suggested in "Before You Begin," maintain a discipline of daily prayer that grows out of the readings and exercises. Review this session guide early in the week to allow adequate time for preparation of its activities. Pray for each participant you expect to be there (and those who may come unexpectedly), and pray for God's Spirit to lead you in your service as group leader.

Offer this or a similar prayer before leading this session:

> *Remind me, O God, of the power you entrust to me as I lead this session, in my relationships with family, friends, and colleagues in vocation. Grant me the wisdom and humility to use that power rightly. In Jesus Christ. Amen.*

Preparing the Room and Materials

On the worship center table, place a candle and matches and a cross or crucifix. Have available a tablet of newsprint and markers in two different colors.

Preparing to Focus

This session aims at helping persons explore how faith brings its witness to bear on powers that impact (and are exercised by) persons and groups in your church and community and the wider world. The texts from the prophets illuminate ways in which issues of power loom large in God's concern for right relationships between individuals and communities and those in authority.

OPENING

- Welcome participants by name. Introduce any guests or visitors to the group.

- On one sheet of newsprint, write "Powers We Live Under." Invite participants to identify powers they live under in the local community, the congregation, the country, and other settings. Write any and all responses at this point.

- On a second sheet of newsprint, write at the top "Powers I Exercise." Ask participants to consider what powers they have over or between others in their families or friendships, in their work, in the church. Again, write all responses.

- Have persons consider how the powers identified on these two (or more) sheets of newsprint rely on truth in enabling their exercise and in identifying their limitations. Explain that this session will be taking a closer look at the interplay between such powers and the witness of faith.

LENTEN EMPHASIS: Invite participants to consider how the
season of Lent narrates encounters by Jesus with "powers"
of various sorts: with religious authorities, with political
authorities, with the "authority" of popular opinion over
what folks expected of Messiah. Discuss how Lent might
confront such established authorities with truth: truth
about God, truth about where genuine power resides, truth
about discipleship.

• Light the candle and offer this or a similar prayer:

> *God whose power comes revealed in suffering, whose truth
> comes incarnate in the life of a servant: open us to your
> power and authority in the whole of life. Guide us in our
> words, in our reflections, in our time together here and in
> our times when we leave this place: that we may consider
> deeply the call to speak truth, when silence or "going along
> to get along" might seem easier. Teach us not to fear power,
> but to know that power and glory belong to you, and in
> that knowledge to trust your empowering of our words and
> lives. In Jesus Christ. Amen.*

INSIGHTS

• Ask the group members to identify their experience of
God's presence and Word in their lives this past week generated through the daily readings and exercises.

  – Allow participants to look over their journals. Afterward,
  have individuals share what spoke most deeply to them.
  Encourage listening that seeks to discern the presence of
  God in each individual's insights.

- If you have a large group (over twelve persons), you may wish to form small groups for this sharing in order to allow deeper conversations.

- Offer your response to this week's readings and exercises to stimulate dialogue.

- After everyone has spoken, invite the whole group to identify patterns or themes that have emerged. If you formed small groups, first ask each one to summarize the sharing that took place within the group.

LENTEN EMPHASIS: Ask participants to draw parallels between these responses and themes to the season of Lent. You may wish return participants to the conversation in the Opening about the powers encountered by Jesus, and how those encounters may shed light on some of the insights and experiences identified here.

EXPLORATIONS

• Explain that the exploration will have a group and individual component.

• Direct attention to the newsprint responses for "Powers We Live Under." Discuss which of those powers are (1) the most influential in your community, and (2) the most controversial in their exercise or acceptance. If at all possible, limit the choices to two per category. It may be that the powers identified in (1) are the same as in (2).

• Invite groups to form around the powers identified in the previous exercise. Let persons choose which group they wish to be part of. The assignment in each group is this: Discuss what faith and Christian community has to do with this particular power. Ask how faith relates to the sorts of issues related in this week's readings and where conflict might arise between this power and the witness of Christian faith. Consider some specific ways in which individuals and your congregation might "speak truth to power."

- Gather the groups back together and report on conversations. Consider passing on some of the suggestions for speaking truth to power to appropriate persons and boards in the congregation.

- Have persons look at the "Powers I Exercise" sheet and silently identify with one of those (or another not listed) that is part of who they are. Recall the emphasis in this week's final reading on our responsibility to exercise power in just and compassionate ways. Lead the participants with these or similar words:

  Close your eyes. Take a deep breath. Clear your mind. Center on that power you exercise among others. As you do, think of persons who rely upon or suffer from the way you exercise it. Picture their faces. Call to mind what you know of their lives. Consider how your exercise of power brings them good or ill. (PAUSE FOR REFLECTION) Think now of how Christ would exercise that power. What words, what actions, what attitudes, would Christ embody? (PAUSE FOR REFLECTION) Imagine now Christ working through you, in what you do and say and instill. Keep that image in mind, for others would see Christ in you, in the exercise of this power. May Christ live in you and through you. (PAUSE FOR REFLECTION) Open your eyes.

Allow persons an opportunity to offer reflections on this exercise. Honor silence.

LENTEN EMPHASIS: In his journey toward the Cross, Jesus did not shrink from speaking truth to power, whether to Caiaphas or Pilate. Rightful authority can become twisted when institutional survival or sacrifice of the innocent hold the day. Likewise, power can never be denied so that its abuse—or responsibilities—only belong to others. No amount of hand washing can remove responsibilities that have been into our keeping for justice and mercy.

CLOSING

- Place the newsprint sheets on or near the worship center. Have persons reflect silently on the relationship between the powers named on the sheets and the powers revealed in the Cross. Invite persons to recall the readings from the prophets this week. Speaking truth to power came in their words, and speaking truth to power came in the Cross, so that we might live more faithfully and speak more truthfully and exercise our powers more humanely.

- Form a circle and offer this or a similar benediction:

   Use our lips to speak your truth, use our lives to show your power. In Jesus Christ. Amen.

- Remind everyone to read daily in Week 4 and to do the related Spiritual Exercises and journal entries. Make announcements about the next meeting (time, place) and other matters for the common good.

Speaking Hope
to Vulnerability

PREPARATION

Preparing Yourself Spiritually

Read Week 4 of *Turn Toward Promise*. Do each of the daily Spiritual Exercises. As you look ahead at this week's preparations and session, remember some time when you found yourself in a position of vulnerability. What gave you hope or comfort in that situation? How has that affected the way in which you tend to persons in such need? As suggested in "Before You Begin," keep a journal based on your reflections upon the readings and experiences of the exercises. Maintain a discipline of daily prayer that grows out of the readings and exercises. Review this session guide early in the week to allow adequate time for preparation of its activities. Pray for each participant you expect to be there (and those who may come unexpectedly), and pray for God's Spirit to lead you in your service as group leader.

Offer this or a similar prayer before leading this session:

> *God of comfort and encouragement, you have borne me through times of weakness. May this time together remind*

us of that gracious caring you bring, that we in turn may
tend to such need. In Jesus Christ. Amen.

Preparing the Room and Materials

Place a candle and matches on the worship center table.

Preparing to Focus

This session will affirm the prophets' declaration of God's presence with and advocacy for those who stand vulnerable in this world. In doing so, the session will also encourage participants not only to claim that promise for their own but to explore ways of being in ministry with the vulnerable among them.

OPENING

- Greet participants by name as they enter. Introduce any guests or visitors to the group.

- Brainstorm ideas on what makes persons vulnerable today. For the moment, do not dwell on "who" the vulnerable are among us but what forces or conditions impose vulnerability on others (or ourselves).

- Pair off participants. Invite each person to share with the partner: (1) a recent personal experience of vulnerability, and (2) what brought hope or strength in that experience. Allow time first for individuals to reflect on this before starting the sharing.

- Afterward, gather the group together and ask: *In what ways did faith, Christian community, or the presence of God figure in that experience shared with your partner?*

LENTEN EMPHASIS: Compassion, whose literal meaning is "to suffer with," marks the journey of Jesus on the way to Jerusalem. In healings, in advocacies (e.g., the woman caught in adultery in John 8), Jesus enters the situations of vulnerable persons in redemptive ways. At times, we find ourselves on the "vulnerable" side of the equation, in need of someone to speak and act on our behalf. At other times, we find ourselves called to the compassion side of the equation, beckoned by Christ to minister as he ministered among us.

- Light the candle and offer this or a similar prayer:

  We are grateful, O God, that you tend to us with mercy and compassion. When we find ourselves vulnerable, we may trust to find you close by. And we are grateful, O God, that you send us out to bear mercy and compassion. When we find others vulnerable, you commission us to bear your presence. Be present to us in this time, that we may learn your gentle grace for us, and how you would have us grace others. In Jesus Christ. Amen.

INSIGHTS

- Ask the group members to identify their experience of God's presence and word in their lives this past week generated through the daily readings and exercises.

  – Give participants a moment to look over their journals. Afterward, have individuals share what spoke most deeply to them. Encourage listening that seeks to discern the presence and movement of God in each individual's insights.

- If you have a large group (over twelve persons), you may wish to form small groups for this sharing in order to allow deeper conversations.

- Offer your response to this week's readings and exercises to stimulate dialogue.

- After everyone has spoken, invite the group to identify patterns or themes that have emerged. If you formed small groups, preface this with a report from each group that summarizes the sharing that took place.

LENTEN EMPHASIS: Ask participants to draw parallels between these responses and themes to the season of Lent. For example, Jesus not only ministered to persons on the way to Jerusalem but found ministry from others (a woman who anointed him, a bystander who responded to his cry of thirst on the cross). How do these words of the prophets not only minister to us in our times of vulnerability, but encourage us to engage in such ministry to others?

EXPLORATIONS

• Direct participants to review the daily Spiritual Exercises from this week. Ask them to identify and select one that: (1) spoke to them most deeply, and/or (2) they would like to spend more time on. Group persons together according to which choice they made (for example, those who selected the exercise for Day One, those who selected the exercise for Day Two, etc.). Do not worry if the groups are not evenly divided or if one or more of the exercises are not represented. If any of the groups have six or more persons, divide them into subgroups (the ideal is to have at least three but no more than five persons per group).

- Explain that each group is to do that Spiritual Exercise *together*. Allow the groups to determine how they will convert the directions to a group exercise. Offer advice as needed, but let them find their way of doing this.

LENTEN EMPHASIS: During the journey to Jerusalem, Jesus spends significant time teaching the disciples not only about his coming suffering but also about the meaning of Christian community and discipleship. Jesus' ministry to the disciples prepared them for their ministries on his behalf. Spiritual formation then, as now, comes not only in personal practices but in the context of group conversations such as your group's experience of this Spiritual Exercise.

- Afterward, gather the groups together and invite them to share their experiences and learnings. Preface the sharing by asking people to comment briefly on doing the Spiritual Exercise in a group compared to doing the exercise independently.

- Invite participants to discuss ways in which these exercises have clarified or raised questions about the meaning of "speaking hope to vulnerability" today, both as recipients of God's gracious presence and as those called upon to show compassion for such persons. Bring the attention of participants back to the opening exercise, where we considered both what makes persons vulnerable today and the participants' own experiences of vulnerability. What connections do they make between those opening conversations and the shared Spiritual Exercises?

CLOSING

- Gather persons around the worship center. Invite individuals to identify what this session has brought to mind or heart. What questions remain? What affirmations will be carried from here?

- Join hands and close in a circle of prayer. Invite participants to name, one at a time, an individual or group who currently experiences vulnerability. After each naming, lead the group in this refrain:

  God of compassion, be with your children. Christ Incarnate, may we embody your presence.

  At the end, close with this prayer:

  We too sometimes pass through the waters. So be with each of us here when we feel alone, when trouble comes, when fears assail. Hold us, as we now hold on to one another. You name us as your children, so may we trust in your sure keeping. For we belong to you and to one another in Jesus Christ. Amen.

- Remind everyone to read daily in Week 5 and to do the related Spiritual Exercises and journal entries. Make announcements about the next meeting (time, place) and other matters for the common good.

Making Room
for Possibilities

PREPARATION

Preparing Yourself Spiritually

Read Week 5 of *Turn Toward Promise*. Do each of the daily Spiritual Exercises. In preparing for this week's theme and readings, recall times when faith has surprised you with some revelation about yourself or your community—or the grace of God! What made it hard to accept that new insight or possibility? How do you keep yourself open to God's possibilities?

As suggested in "Before You Begin," keep a journal based on your reflections upon the readings and experiences of the exercises. Maintain a discipline of daily prayer that grows out of the readings and exercises. Review this session guide early in the week to allow adequate time for preparation of its activities. Pray for each participant you expect to be there (and those who may come unexpectedly), and pray for God's Spirit to lead you in your service as group leader.

Offer this or a similar prayer before leading this session:

> *Save me, O God, from certainty that does not risk surprise.*
> *May your Spirit surprise us in this session with the ways*

you come to us unexpectedly, and with the calls you bring to us we have not heard or noticed before. In Jesus Christ. Amen.

Preparing the Room and Materials

Place a candle and matches on the worship center table. Push the worship table into a corner and crowd all the chairs into another corner in order to create as large an empty space in the usual meeting area as possible. Have paper and pens or pencils available.

Preparing to Focus

This session will explore how the prophets continually push Israel—and the church—to not only consider new possibilities in our life and relationship with God, but to take action that makes room for the breaking in of God's new purposes and workings.

OPENING

- Welcome participants as they enter. Introduce any guests or visitors.

- Direct persons to stand (or get a chair and sit) in the center of the room. Explain they are to crowd in as close as possible to one another.

- Once everyone is packed together, invite persons to relate what comfort or discomfort this "gathering" presents. Ask this question: *If a stranger walked into the room right now, would that person be attracted or put off? Why?* After allowing responses, invite persons to comment on the reasons why making a bit more room might be a good thing. What possibilities would it create?

- Have persons break out of this tight configuration and arrange chairs and worship center as they feel moved to do (if the arrangement is not the usual one, that's fine). If time permits, once everyone is seated, repeat the question about a stranger walking in for silent reflection.

> LENTEN EMPHASIS: *Making room* relates to a spiritual discipline required of Jesus' first disciples on their way toward Jerusalem. Previous ideas about Messiah were challenged by Jesus' teaching on the suffering and dying that awaited him. The disciples had to make room for these new ideas about gaining life in losing it. That must have been startling for them even as it may still be today. Invite participants to reflect on connections between the disciples' experience and participants' experience in the opening activity.

- Call on one of the participants to light the candle as a visible reminder during this and other sessions that we gather in God's presence, seeking God's light for our lives.

- Offer this or a similar prayer:

> *God of Spirit, free to move beyond our expectations, be with us in this time together. Teach us the gift and discipline of following where you would lead, of making room in our attitudes and commitments for your movement and possibilities. In Jesus Christ. Amen.*

INSIGHTS

- Ask the group members to identify their experience of God's presence and word in their lives this past week generated through the daily readings and exercises.

  - Give participants a moment to look over their journals. Afterward, have individuals share what spoke most deeply to them. Encourage listening that seeks to discern the presence and movement of God in each individual's insights.

  - If you have a large group (over twelve persons), you may wish to form small groups for this sharing in order to allow deeper conversations.

  - Offer your response to this week's readings and exercises to stimulate conversation.

  - After everyone has spoken, invite the group to identify patterns or themes that have emerged. If you formed small groups, preface this with a report from each group that summarizes the sharing that took place.

LENTEN EMPHASIS: Ask participants to draw parallels between these responses and themes to the season of Lent. In particular, how does "making room for possibilities" connect with what participants find themselves engaged in during this season of Lent? For example, Jesus surprised disciples on the way to Jerusalem by teaching a suffering Messiah and cross-bearing discipleship. How do the prophets' words this week surprise us in our usual ways of doing things (including church)? How do they suggest we may more readily follow Jesus' new ways?

EXPLORATIONS

- Have persons turn to the Reflection Guide on page 192. Provide pencils or pens for participants who need them and offer blank paper for those who so not wish to write in their book.

- Participants will first work on this Reflection Guide by themselves. Explain that they are to work on at least one, but no more than two, areas in each of the "making room" columns (for example, a person might choose "personal responsibility" in the column "making room in my life for" and "inclusive hospitality" under "making room in our community for").

Encourage persons to use the three reflection questions on the opening page to guide them in each area. They may refer back to the reading and scripture associated with each area, though the emphasis here is on their personal views and understandings. They may make notes in the space provided in the Reflection Guide pages or use blank paper.

Affirm that the core purpose of this activity is to bring the week's theme of "making room for possibilities" to bear on specific situations participants face in their personal lives as well as in the life of the congregation or wider community.

> LENTEN EMPHASIS: Lent provides a season when inner reflection may lead to change and repentance in the whole of life, personal and corporate. Encourage persons to engage with this Reflection Guide as an intentional form of exploring places in their lives and the life of the community where change and new life beckon. Ask them to think about what such transformation might involve.

- Gather the group together. Invite participants to share, as they feel comfortable doing so, some insights or challenges that came to them about making room in their lives. Consider how participants might support one another in that. Move to the reflections on making room in community. Read each category, allowing persons who spent time considering that area to share what they choose. Encourage persons who worked in the same area to consider visiting with their counterparts at a later date on these matters. The group might also identify how and to whom members might convey these ideas and concerns.

- Encourage participants to fill out the rest of the Reflection Guide at a later time. Each category could be done for self or community as a daily Spiritual Exercise, once this series has concluded.

CLOSING

- Allow a time for persons to review this meeting. Helpful questions might include:

    What especially touched your heart and mind?
    When did you feel yourself in the presence of God?

- Remind everyone to read daily in Week 6 and to do the related Spiritual Exercises and journal entries. Make announcements about the next meeting (time, place) and other matters for the common good.

- Invite persons to bring with them some object that symbolizes promise, and to be prepared to offer a brief explanation of its meaning to the group.

- Close with a song that invites persons to make room for the possibilities God has yet to break open in our lives. If singing is not an option, read the words as a litany or responsive reading. For example: "Spirit, Spirit of Gentleness," "Lord, You Have Come to the Lakeshore," "Hymn of Promise" ("In the Bulb, There Is a Flower"), or one of your own choosing.

REFLECTIOп GUIDE

Spend time reflecting on new possibilities for your life and for your community (congregation and/or wider community) in areas identified along the left side of these pages.

In each case, ask yourself the following questions; then make notes in the space provided or on another sheet.

— What is the most pressing issue for me in this area?

— What might need to change?

— How do I sense God leading me in this direction?

Making room in my life for

Making room in our community for

PERSONAL RESPONSIBILITY

Making room in my life for	Making room in our community for

NEW LIFE

FORGIVENESS

TENACITY

**Making room in
my life for**

**Making room in
our community for**

INCLUSIVE HOSPITALITY

FINDING/SERVING GOD
IN NEIGHBOR

Turning Toward Promise

PREPARATION

Preparing Yourself Spiritually

Read Week 6 of *Turn Toward Promise*. Do each of the daily Spiritual Exercises. As you make ready for this last week of preparation, make a list of promises that affect in practical ways how you live your life on a daily basis. How are they connected to your faith?

As suggested in "Before You Begin," keep a journal based on your reflections upon the readings and experiences of the exercises. Maintain a discipline of daily prayer that grows out of the readings and exercises. Review this session guide early in the week to allow adequate time for preparation of its activities. Pray for each participant you expect to be there (and those who may come unexpectedly), and pray for God's Spirit to lead you in your service as group leader.

Offer this or a similar prayer before leading this session:

> *Alpha and Omega, your promises stand before and linger after my life. Renew in us this week the faith to trust those promises, the courage to live in their light, and the grace of finding our promised home in you. In Jesus Christ. Amen.*

Preparing the Room and Materials

Place a candle and matches or lighter on the worship center table. If possible, place the table at the center of your meeting area. If the worship center table is small, provide another table large enough to hold the promise symbols persons have been asked to bring (during the week, you may want to remind group members to bring that symbol with them). Set out pens, pencils, crayons, marking pens, and enough paper for every participant to have at least one sheet.

Preparing to Focus

This session focuses upon the promises of God that sustain us and energize us with hope. The insights of the prophets into the nature and purpose of God's promises will help folks see how those same promises may work in and through us.

OPENING

- Welcome participants as they enter.

- Gather participants in a circle around the worship center table. Have one person light the candle. Ask participants, one at a time, to place their promise symbol on the table in the middle and to say a few words about how that item symbolizes promise to them. If some have forgotten their objects, invite them to identify one thing they might have brought as a symbol and why.

- When all have shared, lead a brief discussion on the importance of promise in our lives, particularly how promises sustain us through unpromising times or experiences. Encourage persons to identify how the symbol they brought has helped them in such moments.

LENTEN EMPHASIS: You will shortly be commemorating Jesus' week of passion and death in Jerusalem. Reflect on what words or promises might have sustained Jesus during that week, or the disciples. Ask participants what promises seem most immediate to them as they prepare to (or already) move through Holy Week.

• Offer this or a similar prayer:

> *In this season of turning, O God, help us to understand in deep ways what it means to turn toward promise: not only for our beliefs, but for our lives and witness. Be present to us in word, in thought, in listening, through this time. Turn us toward promise; turn us toward you. In Jesus Christ. Amen.*

INSIGHTS

• Ask the group members to identify their experience of God's presence and word in their lives this past week generated through the daily readings and exercises.

  – Give participants a moment to look over their journals. Afterward, have individuals share what spoke most deeply to them. Encourage listening that seeks to discern the presence and movement of God in each individual's insights.

  – If you have a large group (over twelve persons), you may wish to form small groups for this sharing in order to allow deeper conversations.

  – Offer your response to this week's readings and exercises, if needed, to stimulate conversation.

– After everyone has spoken, invite the group to identify patterns or themes that have emerged. If you formed small groups, preface this with a report from each group that summarizes the sharing that took place within them.

LENTEN EMPHASIS: Ask participants to draw parallels between these responses and themes to the season of Lent. Invite participants to identify ways in which one of the readings or exercises this week seemed especially helpful in their journeying through Lent and preparing for the remembrances of Maundy Thursday and Good Friday.

EXPLORATIONS

• Distribute paper to participants (at least one sheet per person). Explain that they are to reflect on the promises that sustain them most as persons of faith. They may have encountered these promises during this week's readings and exercises. They may remember promises from childhood or in another time of life. Ask them to identify not simply what that promise is but how it has helped sustained them or their faith community. Ask, *Where do you see God involved in those promises' unfolding now in your life?* The paper is for recording the reflection; participants may write a journal entry or create artwork. Have pens and pencils available for those who write and crayons and marking pens for those who wish to color or draw.

• Invite persons to share what they have written or drawn. Share in small groups if you have more than eight persons. Invite individuals to listen to what others share rather than interpret, comment, or question.

- Say the following or similar words, then allow time for silent reflection:

  Promises are critical to us and to communities, especially faith communities. Promises shape who we say we are, what we do, and why we act. But when times of waiting for promises grow long, we may begin to wonder. We may begin to fall back on trusting only what we can see, measure, or spend. Think now about our community of faith. What changes might a greater or deeper turning toward God's promises mean for us here, together, as a community?

- Invite willing persons to say what came to their minds during this reflection. Explain this is not a time to interpret or critique what others say. Allow one another to offer comments about promise and community.

- When this part of the sharing is completed, ask if folks heard any common directions or themes. Ask, *How might we begin together to orient ourselves more toward promise—and more toward living freed by those promises?* Affirm the promises that empower the group by inviting persons to place the promise papers on the worship table.

LENTEN EMPHASIS: Share these or similar words: *Initially the journey through Holy Week fragmented community. When crisis came, disciples fled into the night—or denied their connections to Jesus. Promises seemed a long way off, as did community. But community re-formed in the light of Christ's raising and in the promise of the Spirit's leading. When scattered followers turned toward promise, God breathed new life into community. How might reflecting on that experience of the disciples empower our own community to turn toward promise in new ways?*

CLOSING

- Form a circle around the worship center and join hands. Thank folks for the time and commitment they have shared in being part of this study. Invite persons to reflect on this group experience over the past six weeks—learnings, experiences, questions, other thoughts. Allow for a time of thanksgiving, which you initiate, that affirms the gifts brought to the group by the participants.

- Close with this prayer offered in unison:

  Holy God, whose promises can be trusted, whose presence guides us through times of crisis, leading us toward hope: we thank you for prophets, in times ancient and present, who point us to you. May their example of truth-telling, whether in refusing to back away from things we would rather not see and admit, or in refusing to yield the hope that is theirs—and ours—in God, give courage to us as we seek to live faithfully in our day. We thank you for those with whom we have shared this journey over these past weeks and pray now that you would guide us in the journey set out before us. We pray this in the name of Christ, who is our judge and our advocate, our truth and our hope. Amen.

- Invite individuals to take their symbols of promise with them as they leave, as a sign of continuing to live beyond this circle as individuals and as a people of God's promises.

About the Author

John Indermark lives in Naselle, Washington, with his wife, Judy, an E-911 dispatcher. Ordained in the United Church of Christ, John served as a parish pastor for sixteen years before developing a ministry of writing that is now his full-time vocation.

Besides devotional and spiritual formation books published by Upper Room Books, John's publications include Christian education curricula for Seasons of the Spirit, The Present Word, New International Lectionary Annual, and Great Themes of the Bible. He has published articles in *The Clergy Journal* and *Exchange* (a publication of the United Church of Canada). He and his son, Jeff, a counselor at a juvenile detention center, have coauthored two study books for young adults published by the Presbyterian Church (USA).

In their spare time, John and Judy enjoy walking the area's logging roads and trails, puttering in their gardens, and exploring Victoria and Vancouver Island.

Other Books by John Indermark

NEGLECTED VOICES
Biblical Spirituality in the Margins

The Bible features many voices of faith, including those whose lives are well-chronicled and those who are mere footnotes in biblical history. In *Neglected Voices*, Indermark explores the lives of lesser known biblical figures who have much to teach us about the importance of faithfulness in all places and times. (ISBN 0-8358-0891-2; separate leader's guide, 0-8358-0890-4)

GENESIS OF GRACE
A Lenten Book of Days

Genesis of Grace leads us to a deeper understanding of God's grace by tracing it through the familiar stories of Genesis. Daily reflective readings explore the theme of God's forgiveness as revealed in such stories as the Creation, the Flood, Cain and Abel, and Abraham and Sarah. (ISBN 0-8358-0843-2; separate leader's guide, 0-8358-0844-0)

SETTING THE CHRISTMAS STAGE
Readings for the Advent Season

Advent brings a rush of activities that often makes the pre-Christmas season lose its spiritual meaning. Using the device of a Christmas pageant to examine the biblical revelation, Indermark helps readers connect the biblical stories with their spiritual journeys. *Setting the Christmas Stage* helps readers refocus and thoughtfully consider the characters and places of the season as these impact the spiritual journey. (ISBN 0-8358-0947-1, leader's guide included)

Traveling the Prayer Paths of Jesus

Join Jesus in places of prayer and learn from the daily readings that examine Jesus' prayers in six different settings: out of solitude; by the roadside; on the mountainside; in the upper room; at the garden; upon the cross. An exercise for spiritual formation and a prayer follow each daily reading. The book includes a leader's guide for a six-week, small-group study. (ISBN 0-8358-9857-1)

Companions in Christ
The Way of Grace

This fourth release in the Companions in Christ small-group series invites participants to travel with eight biblical characters (or groups of characters) who discover God's grace through their encounters with Jesus. The resource is more than a survey of the biblical stories. It is a transforming interaction with the events and the characters. And it is an invitation for participants to open their hearts to a deeper knowing of God's grace. (ISBN 0-8358-0843-2)

These books are available through your
local bookstore or you may order directly from
Upper Room Books
1-800-972-0433
online at www.upperroom.org

EVERY DAY
Find a Way

Join with Christians around the world who read and pray—every day.

The Upper Room is a daily devotional guide that unites nearly three million Christians around the world into a global Christian community.

If you are searching for ways to deepen your relationship with God, *The Upper Room* is the ideal devotional guide. It encourages Bible reading, prayer, and meditation—practices that help you grow in the faith. Each day's devotion offers a Bible verse, suggested Bible reading, prayer, prayer focus, and thought for the day. Plus, there's a discussion guide for small groups to use. It's the most versatile, economical resource available for church groups or daily devotional practice.

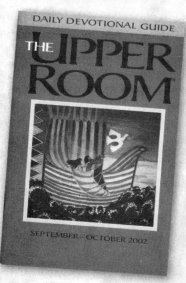

DAILY DEVOTIONAL GUIDE

THE UPPER ROOM

SEPTEMBER–OCTOBER 2002

To order individual subscriptions, call
1-800-925-6847

To order standing orders for groups, call
1-800-972-0433

Visit us online today!
www.upperroom.org